Time Mastery Blueprint

Unleashing Success Through Effective Time Management

DAMIEN SOITOUT

DEDICATION

I dedicate this book to everyone facing the same challenge I have faced when starting in the world. Time management freed me, my companies, employees and partners from falling behind; and everyone should be so lucky as to understanding how to face this very crucial threat when doing business.

CONTENTS

Acknowledgments — i

Preface — 1

1 The Power of Time:
Understanding the Psychology of Time Management — 4

2 Unlocking Your Productivity Potential:
Identifying and Overcoming Time Wasters — 29

3 Prioritizing with Purpose:
Mastering the Art of Task Management — 50

4 From Chaos to Clarity:
Organizing Your Time and Space for Maximum Efficiency — 57

5 The Power of Delegation and Collaboration: Achieving
Exponential Growth Through Effective Teamwork — 73

6 The Art of Saying No:
Setting Boundaries and Protecting Your Time — 91

7 Making Time for What Matters:
Goal Setting and Time Allocation Strategies — 99

8 Building Routines and Rituals:
Establishing Habits for Sustainable Time Management — 108

9 From Procrastination to Action:
Overcoming Resistance and Boosting Motivation — 117

10 The Time-Productivity Connection:
Understanding the Science of Peak Performance — 123

11 Time as a Resource:
Leveraging Technology and Tools for Time Optimization — 135

About the Author — 145

ACKNOWLEDGMENTS

I had not thought about Time Management in a very long time (ironically), and I want to thank my friend and partner Harold, as well as Andy for pointing at a situation where I found myself confronted to it after so many years not paying enough attention to it.

PREFACE

Welcome to the Time Mastery Blueprint, a comprehensive guide that will empower you to master the art of time management in our fast-paced and demanding world. In this Quick Guide, we will dive deep into the psychology behind effective time management and explore the strategies employed by successful individuals to optimize their time and build thriving businesses.

The journey of building a successful business is filled with challenges, opportunities, and constant change. However, the key factor that sets apart successful entrepreneurs and business leaders is their ability to manage time effectively. They recognize that time is a precious resource that, when utilized wisely, can drive productivity, foster growth, and lead to outstanding achievements.

Throughout the chapters of this Quick Guide, we will address specific aspects of time management, offering insights and practical techniques to help you overcome common challenges. From the importance of time management to assessments that evaluate your current approach, we will provide you with valuable advice and analysis to enhance your time management skills.

Understanding the psychology behind procrastination, multitasking, and prioritization is crucial, and we will equip you with the necessary tools to overcome these obstacles. With real-life examples, detailed analysis, and actionable advice, you will be able to implement effective time management strategies in your daily life and achieve tangible results.

It is important to acknowledge that time management is not a one-size-fits-all solution. Each individual and business has unique needs and circumstances. Therefore, this Quick Guide offers a range of strategies and techniques, allowing you to tailor them to your specific requirements and objectives. Whether you are an aspiring entrepreneur, a small business owner, or a seasoned executive, the principles and insights shared within these pages will unlock your full potential and help you create a thriving business.

The knowledge and wisdom contained within these chapters are designed to empower you to seize control of your time, maximize productivity, and achieve the success you envision.

Remember, time is a precious asset. By investing it wisely and harnessing its power, you can accomplish extraordinary feats. So, join us on this transformative journey, embrace the principles of effective time management, and let the psychology behind it propel you toward building the thriving business of your dreams.

Best wishes on your quest for success!

Damien Soitout

CHAPTER 1

THE POWER OF TIME: UNDERSTANDING THE PSYCHOLOGY OF TIME MANAGEMENT

Let's embark on a journey to explore the fundamental nature of time and its profound impact on our lives. By understanding the psychology behind time management, we can unlock the secrets to building a thriving business. This chapter provides assessments, detailed analysis, and valuable advice to help you harness the power of time and optimize your productivity.

Time is a Finite Resource

To comprehend the significance of time management, it is crucial to recognize that time is a finite resource. Consider the following questions to assess your perception of time's value:

1. Do you often find yourself saying, "There is not enough time in the day"?

Trying to rationalize this state of mind is the wrong way to go. I recently came across a single mother of two young children who started her business while nursing one of them, and having to drive around town to take the eldest child to school and other activities. Her day has the same twenty-four hours as everyone else; her responsibilities span beyond her own needs as two little boys depend on her, yet, she has successfully built a business she can live from, save money from, and she can even invest and travel on the money she makes from it.

Every single successful entrepreneur possesses the same amount of time in a day, week, month or year. It is time to organize yours and quit thinking as an everyday person.

2. Are you aware of the limited number of hours available to accomplish your goals?

In the above question, I purposefully omitted one key aspect of this young mother's day. Not only hers, as a matter of fact, but the same applies to all people: we may have twenty-four hours in a day, but we need to sleep, eat, exercise, relax… What matters most isn't just optimizing your day based on the full clock, but determining how much free time you really own out of all your other obligations in order to make your dream come true.

3. Do you prioritize your tasks and allocate time accordingly?

Prioritizing tasks means quitting the to-do list system. Instead of planning based on what comes first on your desk, you must learn to work with what I call a MAP: Massive Action Plan.

It is a file which organizes objectives in chunks of tasks, sorted by importance, so that one done objective unlocks the next one. As Jay Papasan and Gary Keller say in their book "The ONE Thing", if you chase two rabbits at once, you won't catch either one. Learn to focus on the most important item of the day, and once accomplished, celebrate it before moving on to the next one.

Recognizing time as a finite resource is the first step towards effective time management. Each day presents us with a fixed number of hours, and how we choose to utilize them determines our success. By understanding the value of time, you can cultivate a mindset that prioritizes tasks, allocates time strategically, and maximizes productivity.

Time Perception and its Influence

Our perception of time can vary greatly, affecting our behavior, decision-making, and productivity. Reflect on the following questions to assess your time perception:

1. Do you find that time passes quickly or slowly depending on the task or situation?

The perception of time can vary depending on the task or situation due to several factors.

a. Attention and engagement: When we are fully engaged and absorbed in an activity or task, our attention is focused on the present moment. This heightened state of concentration can make time seem to fly by because we are less aware of the passage of time.

b. Novelty and stimulation: New or exciting experiences tend to grab our attention and make us more conscious of the passing of time. When we encounter novel situations, our brain processes more information, leading to a sense that time is slowing down.

c. Boredom and monotony: Conversely, repetitive or monotonous tasks can make time feel like it is dragging. When we are bored or not mentally stimulated, our attention may wander, and we become more aware of the passage of time.

d. Memory and perception: Our perception of time is influenced by how our memories are formed and retrieved. When we reflect back on an event or experience, our memory plays a role in shaping our perception of its duration. If the event was memorable and filled with meaningful experiences, it may seem like it lasted longer.

e. Emotional state: Our emotions can significantly affect our perception of time. In high-stress situations, time can feel compressed, and events may seem to unfold rapidly. On the other hand, during moments of relaxation or enjoyment, time can appear to slow down.

f. Time estimation and cognitive load: When we are actively engaged in estimating the duration of an activity, our cognitive load increases. This heightened awareness of time can make it feel like it is passing more slowly.

It is important to note that these factors can interact with each other and vary from person to person. Therefore, different individuals may experience the passage of time differently in the same task or situation.

2. Are you aware of how your mindset and engagement with a task influence your perception of time?

Becoming aware of how your mindset and engagement with a task influence your perception of time involves practicing self-reflection and mindfulness. Here are some strategies to help you develop this awareness:

a. Mindfulness meditation: Engage in regular mindfulness meditation practices. By focusing your attention on the present moment without judgment, you can become more attuned to your thoughts, emotions, and bodily sensations. This increased self-awareness can help you recognize how your mindset and engagement impact your perception of time.

b. Reflect on past experiences: Take time to reflect on past tasks or activities and how you perceived the passage of time during those moments. Were there specific factors that made time seem to fly by or drag? Were you fully engaged or distracted? By analyzing these experiences, you can gain insights into the relationship between your mindset, engagement, and time perception.

c. Monitor your attention: During different tasks or activities, pay attention to the quality and intensity of your focus. Notice when your mind wanders or becomes fully absorbed.

Assess how your level of engagement affects your perception of time. This self-monitoring can help you recognize patterns and understand how your mindset influences time perception.

4. Embrace variety and novelty

Engage in a variety of tasks or activities that stimulate your mind and senses. Novel experiences tend to create a heightened awareness of time. By intentionally seeking out new challenges and incorporating variety into your daily routine, you can expand your perception of time and make it feel richer and more memorable.

d. Practice time estimation: Try estimating the duration of tasks or activities before checking the actual time. Compare your estimates to the actual time taken. Over time, you'll develop a better understanding of how your engagement level and mindset impact your ability to accurately estimate time.

e. Cultivate a positive mindset: Approach tasks with a positive and open mindset. When you enjoy what you're doing or have a positive attitude, time can feel more fluid and enjoyable. Emphasize the intrinsic value or purpose of the task, rather than solely focusing on the end result. This shift in mindset can positively influence your time perception.

Remember that individual experiences can vary, and it may take time and practice to develop a deeper awareness of how your mindset and engagement influence your perception of time.

3. Do you make conscious efforts to optimize your experience of time?

To make conscious efforts to optimize your experience of time, consider the following strategies:

a. Set clear goals: Define specific and achievable goals for your tasks and activities. Having a clear sense of purpose and direction can help you stay focused and motivated, making your experience of time more fulfilling.

b. Prioritize and manage your time: Identify your priorities and allocate your time accordingly. Use time management techniques such as creating to-do lists, setting deadlines, and breaking tasks into smaller, manageable chunks. This structured approach can enhance your productivity and reduce the feeling of time slipping away.

c. Practice time blocking: Allocate dedicated blocks of time for specific tasks or activities. By creating designated time slots for focused work, relaxation, exercise, and other aspects of your life, you can establish a better balance and make the most of each moment.

d. *Minimize distractions*: Identify and minimize potential distractions that can disrupt your focus and prolong the time taken for tasks. Consider turning off notifications on your electronic devices, finding a quiet environment, or using productivity tools that help limit distractions.

e. *Use time wisely during transitions*: Use transitional periods, such as commuting or waiting in line, to engage in activities that are meaningful or enjoyable. This can include reading, listening to educational podcasts, practicing mindfulness, or simply taking a moment to reflect and recharge.

f. *Practice single-tasking*: Avoid multitasking and instead focus on one task at a time. By giving your full attention to each activity, you can enhance your engagement, productivity, and overall satisfaction with the passage of time.

g. *Take breaks and rest*: Incorporate regular breaks into your schedule to recharge and rejuvenate. Research suggests that taking short breaks can improve focus and productivity. Additionally, ensure you prioritize sufficient rest and sleep to maintain optimal cognitive functioning and well-being.

h. *Cultivate mindfulness*: Practice being fully present and engaged in the current moment. Mindfulness can help you appreciate the richness of your experiences, reduce stress, and heighten your awareness of the passage of time.

i. Reflect and learn from your experiences: Regularly reflect on how you spend your time and evaluate what works well for you. Consider what activities bring you joy, fulfillment, and a sense of time well-spent. Use these insights to make adjustments and optimize your future time management.

Remember that optimizing your experience of time is a personal journey, and it may require experimentation and adaptation to find strategies that work best for you. Stay open to exploring different approaches and be willing to adjust your routines as needed.

Time perception is subjective and influenced by various factors such as engagement, focus, and enjoyment of a task. By cultivating a sense of mindfulness and being present in the moment, you can enhance your time perception. This awareness allows you to gauge your progress, identify patterns, and make necessary adjustments to your schedule, ultimately optimizing your experience of time and increasing productivity.

Time and Decision-Making

Time plays a vital role in decision-making, particularly in terms of task prioritization and resource allocation. Of course, decision-making depends on more than time, however, many great businesses have failed due to time-related issues: timing, and timing. What does it mean? It means either the timing was not right to launch a particular product or service in the time-period. Or the timing to get things rolling was too slow and they lost the opportunity to be the first on the market offering what they were getting ready to launch. Thousands of business ideas fail from the get-go because of these issues. And the one way to palliate to this issue for anyone, is improving your decision-making by applying some simple time-based rules towards its process. After years of failing and succeeding at many crazy business ideas, some questions arose which helped create a working pattern when it was time to make a decision. You can evaluate your decision-making process with the following questions:

1. Do you consider the time required for each task when making decisions?

Are you being realistic, clear, aware, or all of the above, when applying a timeframe to a task. It is rather mandatory to have full transparency and awareness of the challenges to come, and even maybe over evaluate the time you will really need to accomplish what you set your mind to.

2. Are you mindful of the trade-offs involved in allocating time to different activities?

This is particularly important as most entrepreneurs tend to try and do everything, or many things, alone and at once. It makes sense, cost-wise, time-wise, focus-wise it might seem like a good idea. Yet, a quick analysis will probably demonstrate that you will have to sacrifice one or the other thing, or at least quality of a result for another, when allocating time to more than one objective at once.

3. Do you utilize effective decision-making models to optimize your time allocation?

What are decision-making models? There are several effective decision-making models that can help optimize your time allocation. Here are a few commonly used ones:

a. Eisenhower Matrix: The Eisenhower Matrix, also known as the Urgent-Important Matrix, helps prioritize tasks based on their urgency and importance. It divides tasks into four categories:

(a) Urgent and important,

(b) Important but not urgent,

(c) Urgent but not important, and

(d) Not urgent and not important.

By categorizing tasks, you can focus on high-priority activities and delegate or eliminate non-essential ones.

b. Pareto Principle (80/20 Rule): The Pareto Principle states that roughly 80% of the results come from 20% of the efforts. Apply this principle by identifying the key tasks or activities that contribute the most to your desired outcomes. Allocate more time and energy to these high-impact tasks to maximize your productivity and achieve significant results.

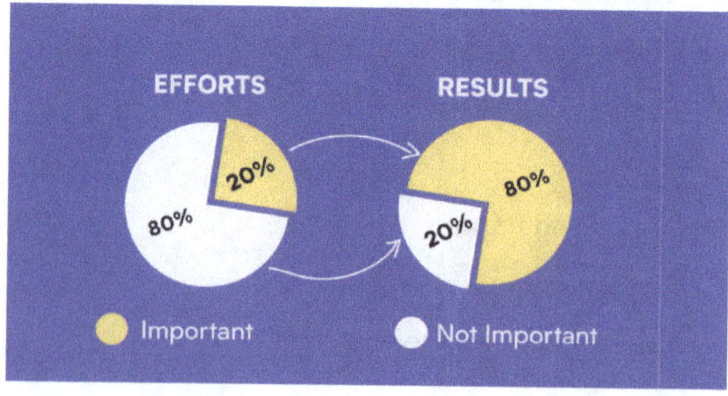

c. Decision Matrix: A decision matrix involves creating a table that assesses different options based on multiple criteria. Assign weights to each criterion to reflect its importance, and rate each option accordingly. By systematically evaluating and comparing alternatives, you can make more informed decisions about how to allocate your time effectively.

Example of a Decision Matrix

	Safety Risk	Inflation Risk	Rate of Return	Management Difficulty	Stability	Compatibility With Current Business	Totals
Real Estate Rentals	9	7	5	9	9	9	112.5
Blimpie Franchise	5	6	4	3	6	9	74.0
Carpet Cleaning Business	3	6	4	3	5	9	64.5
Note Buying Business	6	8	6	6	7	9	97.5
Retail Convenience Store	4	4	3	3	6	9	61.0
Business Consultant	9	5	4	6	8	9	96.0
Investment Advisor	7	7	9	6	7	7	105.5
Web Designer	7	5	5	6	7	6	86.5
Lifestyle Consultant	6	4	7	6	6	9	87.0
Travel Specialist	6	7	7	6	5	9	94.5
Internet Business	8	7	9	8	7	8	114.5
Weight	4	3	3	2	1.5	1	

d. Cost-Benefit Analysis: Cost-Benefit Analysis involves considering the potential costs and benefits of different choices. Assess the advantages and disadvantages, both in terms of time and other resources, associated with each option. This analysis helps you identify the choices that offer the greatest benefits while minimizing potential drawbacks.

B5	f_x	=B3/B2

	A	
1	Particulars	
2	Total Value of the Costs from the Project	$10
3	Benefits Available from the Project	$21
4		
5	Benefit Cost Ratio	$2.1
6		

Benefit- Cost Ratio = Benefits available from the project / Total value of Costs

*e. **RACI Matrix***: The RACI Matrix is particularly useful for team-based projects or collaborative efforts. It clarifies roles and responsibilities by categorizing tasks into Responsible, Accountable, Consulted, and Informed roles. This model ensures effective time allocation by clearly defining who is responsible for each task and who needs to be consulted or informed.

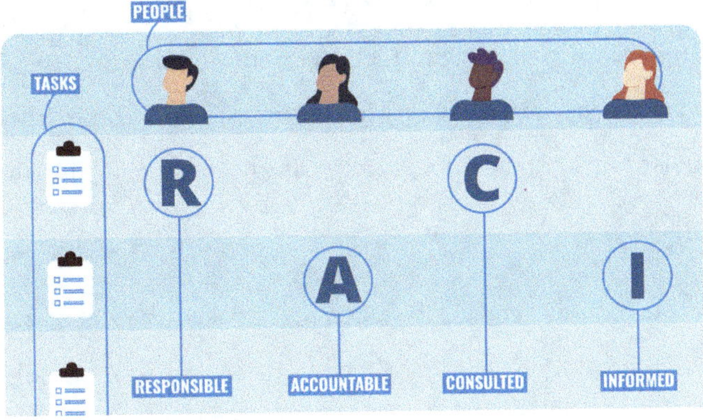

f. Eat That Frog: Popularized by Brian Tracy, the "Eat That Frog" approach suggests tackling the most challenging or important task first thing in the morning. By completing the most difficult task early, you build momentum, increase productivity, and free up mental space for other activities throughout the day.

Remember, the effectiveness of decision-making models can vary depending on the context and individual preferences. Experiment with different models, adapt them to your specific needs, and find the approach that works best for you in optimizing your time allocation.

Time scarcity necessitates making conscious choices about task prioritization. By incorporating time considerations into your decision-making process, you can allocate resources effectively, ensure important tasks receive appropriate attention, and prevent time-related conflicts. Various decision-making models, such as the Eisenhower Matrix (or the ABCDE method), can assist in prioritizing tasks based on their urgency and importance.

*****

Time Awareness and Reflection

Developing time awareness is essential for effective time management. Evaluate your level of time awareness with the following questions:

1. Do you reflect on how you spend your time and its alignment with your goals?

Everyone things launching a new project will take time off some of their habits and usual activities. It sounds fair enough. Now, ask those who actually took the step towards a new challenge such as launching a business. They will take a second to remember who they were before, and identify every single thing they sacrificed in order to become who they are in this moment, to actually become successful.

The lesson you should learn from this question isn't what you are doing right for your project. It is everything you do wrong. Every single second spent on something which brings no value or progress to your project.

It could be anything from watching Netflix every night for 2 hours, to spending 3 hours cooking in the afternoon, to driving in traffic 2 hours per day. Anything that brings no value to your goals should be removed from your daily life. It seems drastic, but after failing eleven times, barely recuperating the money invested initially, I understood something needed to change.

First step was to stop wasting weekends, two days of my week, or 28.57% of my week doing nothing or partying; using these days of nonchalance to be productive when everyone else stay on the sideline.

Second, was to find ways to sleep less, gathering more energy through better diet and higher quality sleep, and removing distractions like TV from my life. I haven't owned or watched TV in over a decade. These little sacrifices, coupled with bigger ones along the journey, helped me built business that will last probably longer than me.

2. Are you aware of patterns or habits that may contribute to time inefficiencies?

TV, movies, restaurants with friends, dating, chatting online, partying and many more activities are actually incompatible with a healthy business. At first anyways. The goal will always be to build something that will allow you to live the way you wish, once it works on its own. But remember that when you start it up, this baby will depend on you to survive every single step of the way. It will require every second of free time available, which means you will have to sacrifice non-essential activities in order for this newborn to have a shot at becoming a toddler, and then a child, then a teen, and maybe even become a strong and independent adult that will thrive without you.

3. Do you regularly review and adjust your schedule based on your time awareness?

When you are aware of your time, you are aware that nothing goes according to plan. It is your job to adjust accordingly. An entrepreneur needs to be flexible, because every external factor is a probable cause for change. Small or big.

Time awareness allows you to evaluate your time utilization and make informed adjustments. Reflecting on your time allocation, identifying patterns, and recognizing time-wasting habits empowers you to make proactive changes. Regularly reviewing and adjusting your schedule ensures that your time aligns with your goals, optimizing productivity and success.

Time Pressure and Stress Management

The passage of time can induce feelings of pressure and stress. You will need to learn to deal with this if you really want your startup to have a chance at becoming something you can earn a living from. There are many ways to deal with stress, and many ways to reduce the amount generated by your activity. You will never be stress free. That is the reason why it is imperative for you to learn how to manage it.

Reflect on the following questions to assess your approach to time-related anxiety:

1. Do you frequently experience stress due to time-related pressures?

If you answer yes, it is normal. There are different levels of yes, however. Maybe you haven't implemented the right decision-making system in your daily routine? Or maybe you haven't established well enough the MAP to follow in order to progress properly on the path of your startup launch. Or maybe you are prone to being stressed easily, and you might need to practice meditation, follow some psychology seminars targeting entrepreneurs, or some other form of mind-bending experiences which can help you find the right way to focus and organize your priorities.

2. Are you able to maintain a calm and focused mindset in the face of tight deadlines?

In other words, do you have the guts to pull a hail Mary out of your hat when the circumstances need it? If you not, you might want to revisit the transparency and self-honesty step of building a timeline for your project. Do not be over-eager. Remember that deadlines are everywhere, but when you set them for yourself, it should not be a debilitating stress inducing task. A tight deadline should always be motivational. Review the way you analyze and set timeframes for your tasks, and maybe you will reduce the stress-inducing items on your MAP.

3. Do you employ stress management techniques to mitigate time-related stress?

If you frequently experience stress due to time-related pressures, here are some strategies you can try to alleviate the stress:

a. Prioritize and delegate: Assess your tasks and responsibilities to determine what truly needs to be done and what can be delegated or eliminated. Focus on high-priority tasks that align with your goals and values, and consider seeking assistance or delegating tasks that can be handled by others.

b. Break tasks into smaller steps: Large and overwhelming tasks can contribute to time-related stress. Break them down into smaller, more manageable steps, like in a MAP. This approach helps you focus on one task at a time, reduces the feeling of being overwhelmed, and allows for better time allocation.

c. Set realistic goals and expectations: Be realistic and honest with yourself in setting your goals and deadlines. Avoid overloading yourself with too many tasks within a limited timeframe. By setting achievable expectations, you reduce the pressure and stress associated with time-related pressures.

d. Time management techniques: Utilize effective time management techniques such as creating schedules, a MAP, and prioritizing tasks. Use tools such as calendars, planners, or time-tracking apps to help you stay organized and focused. These techniques can provide a sense of structure and control, reducing stress.

e. Practice self-care: Take care of your physical and mental well-being. Engage in activities that help you relax and recharge, such as exercise, meditation, hobbies, or spending time with loved ones. Prioritizing self-care reduces stress levels and enhances your ability to manage time effectively.

f. Learn to say no: It is important to recognize your limits and be comfortable saying no when necessary. Overcommitting can lead to feeling overwhelmed and stressed. Assess requests and obligations carefully, and learn to decline or negotiate when your time and energy are already stretched thin.

g. Seek support and communicate: Reach out to others for support or guidance. Share your concerns with trusted friends, family, or colleagues who can offer perspective, advice, or assistance. Effective communication can help alleviate stress by sharing the workload or gaining new insights on time management.

h. Practice stress management techniques: Employ stress management techniques such as deep breathing, mindfulness, or engaging in activities that help you relax and reduce stress. These techniques can improve your ability to cope with time-related pressures and maintain a calmer mindset.

If you find that time-related stress persists and significantly affects your well-being or productivity, consider seeking professional help from a therapist or counselor who can provide personalized strategies and support.

Time pressure and stress can negatively impact productivity and well-being. By implementing stress management techniques such as prioritization, time blocking, delegation, and setting realistic expectations, you can mitigate time-related stress. Cultivating a calm and focused mindset allows you to navigate tight deadlines with clarity and composure, ultimately enhancing productivity and overall success.

To build a thriving business, mastering time management is crucial. Consider the following advice to harness the power of time:

1. Recognize time as a finite resource and prioritize tasks accordingly.

2. Cultivate mindfulness and engagement to optimize your perception of time.

3. Incorporate time considerations into your decision-making process.

4. Develop time awareness through reflection and adjustment of your schedule.

5. Employ stress management techniques to mitigate time-related stress.

By embracing these principles and applying them to your business endeavors, you can unlock the secrets of successful time management. Stay tuned as we dive deeper into the realm of time mastery in the subsequent chapters, providing you with practical strategies and insights to build a thriving business through effective time management.

CHAPTER 2

UNLOCKING YOUR PRODUCTIVITY POTENTIAL: IDENTIFYING & OVERCOMING TIME WASTERS

We live in a world filled with distractions, and it is crucial to understand how they impact our time and productivity. By identifying and eliminating these time wasters, you can unlock your true potential and optimize your output. Let's explore the assessments, details, and analysis to help you reclaim your time and achieve greater productivity.

Multitasking and its Limitations

One of the most prevalent misconceptions about productivity is the notion of multitasking. Many individuals believe that engaging in multiple tasks simultaneously allows for increased efficiency. However, scientific research has consistently shown that our brains are not wired for multitasking. In fact, attempting to juggle multiple tasks leads to decreased productivity, increased errors, and a loss of focus. To assess your reliance on multitasking, consider the following questions:

1. Do you find yourself frequently switching between tasks?

In the first place, ask yourself why you are multitasking between these tasks instead of finishing one and moving on to the next. It is possible at times that a few tasks depend on one another, but in this case, you should consider using what is called "task batching".

This is the concept of grouping similar tasks together and allocating dedicated blocks of time to work on them.

For example, set aside specific time slots for responding to emails, making phone calls, or working on specific projects. This approach reduces the need for constant task-switching and allows for better concentration and efficiency.

It is possible you over-sorted out tasks, and some must be dealt with together. If this is not the case, review your tasks' priority levels. Maybe you need to readjust your initial analysis.

2. Are you easily distracted by external stimuli while working on important projects?

Create an environment that minimizes distractions. Silence notifications on your electronic devices, close unnecessary tabs or applications on your computer, and find a quiet space to work. By reducing distractions, you can stay more engaged and focused on the task at hand.

3. Have you noticed a decline in the quality of your work due to multitasking?

Multitasking can be mandatory in some instances of work; however, you must learn to manage it. A few techniques exist precisely to make it easier on you, to improve the quality of the results obtained from the time spent on each task, and for you not to get demotivated by the amount of work required by these specifics items on your list.

a. Use time-blocking techniques: Allocate specific time blocks for different activities and stick to the schedule. During each block, commit to working solely on the designated task without interruptions. This structured approach helps you maintain focus and discourages frequent task-switching.

b. _Implement the Pomodoro Technique_: The Pomodoro Technique involves working in focused intervals, typically 15 to 25 minutes, followed by short breaks. Set a timer for a specific interval, work on a single task during that time, and then take a short break. This method helps improve concentration and provides a structured rhythm for your work.

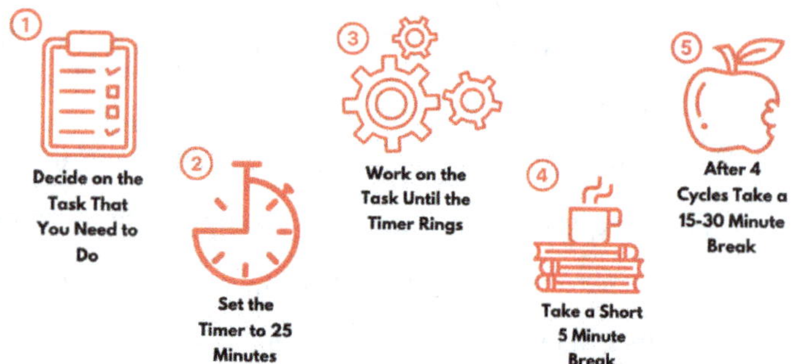

c. _Improve time estimation_: Accurately estimate the time required for each task or activity. By having a realistic understanding of how long a task will take, you can allocate sufficient time and avoid the need to switch tasks prematurely. This is possible by having a real understanding of the work at hand, usually learned from experience. If you find it difficult to estimate how long a task will take, try to use the Pomodoro Technique.

d. Develop self-awareness: Pay attention to your own tendencies and triggers for task-switching. Notice when you feel the urge to switch tasks and explore the underlying reasons behind it.

Are you:

- seeking novelty?

- feeling overwhelmed?

- avoiding a challenging task?

Understanding these patterns can help you develop strategies to address them effectively.

e. Use productivity tools: Consider utilizing productivity tools or apps that can help you manage tasks and stay focused. These programs often provide features such as task lists, reminders, and progress tracking, which can enhance your organization and keep you on track.

Multitasking divides our attention and compromises the quality of our output. The brain requires time to refocus and adjust when switching between tasks, resulting in cognitive load and reduced efficiency.

To overcome this challenge, it is essential to cultivate a practice of focused attention and deep work. By dedicating uninterrupted blocks of time to specific tasks, you can harness your cognitive resources more effectively, resulting in higher quality work.

*****

Digital Distractions and Technological Temptations

In today's digital age, technology plays a significant role in our lives. While it offers numerous benefits, it also presents a considerable source of distraction. Assess your relationship with technology using the following questions:

1. Do you frequently check your smartphone or other devices for notifications?

a. Disable non-essential notifications: Review the notifications settings on your devices and disable or limit notifications for non-essential apps.

Prioritize notifications from important contacts or apps related to your work, while minimizing distractions from social media or entertainment apps.

b. Use notification management features: If you do not wish completely disable notifications, many devices have built-in features that allow you to manage them effectively.

For example, you can use "Do Not Disturb" mode during focused work periods to silence notifications or schedule specific times for uninterrupted work.

Take advantage of these features to create a distraction-free environment.

2. Are you easily drawn into social media feeds or other online distractions?

In today's digital age, the constant barrage of information and entertainment online can be captivating, often leading us down the rabbit hole of social media feeds and other diversions.

It is essential to reflect on whether you easily become absorbed in these online platforms, potentially hindering your focus and productivity in other areas of life. Consider the impact of these distractions on your time management and overall well-being.

3. Do you struggle to disconnect from technology during work hours?

Digital distractions disrupt our workflow, consume valuable time, and hinder productivity. The constant notifications, social media updates, and online temptations divert our attention, leading to fragmented focus and reduced output.

To combat these distractions, it is crucial to implement strategies that manage your digital environment. Consider setting specific boundaries, such as designating specific times to check notifications or utilizing productivity tools that block or limit access to distracting apps and websites.

Procrastination and Overcoming Resistance

Procrastination is a common challenge that can significantly hinder productivity. Assess your propensity for procrastination by reflecting on the following questions:

1. Do you frequently postpone tasks or delay starting important projects?

2. Are you easily swayed by distractions or excuses that prevent you from taking action?

3. Do you find it difficult to stay motivated and overcome resistance when faced with challenging tasks?

Procrastination stems from various underlying factors, including fear of failure, perfectionism, or a lack of clarity about the task at hand.

Understanding the root causes of procrastination is essential for developing effective strategies to overcome it. By employing techniques such as:

- breaking tasks into smaller ones,

- manageable steps,

- utilizing time-blocking methods,

- and leveraging accountability systems,

you can conquer procrastination and enhance your productivity.

Internal Distractions and Self-Management

In addition to external distractions, internal factors such as thoughts, emotions, and habits can significantly impact productivity. Reflect on the following questions to assess your self-management skills:

1. Are you easily overwhelmed by negative thoughts or emotions while working?

The ability to manage and cope with negative thoughts or emotions while working is a crucial aspect of personal well-being and professional success. People vary in their susceptibility to being overwhelmed by negative thoughts or emotions during work. Several factors can contribute to this, including the nature of the job, personal resilience, and external stressors. Here are some strategies that individuals often find helpful in navigating and mitigating negative thoughts or emotions in the workplace:

Mindfulness and Meditation: Incorporating mindfulness techniques or short meditation breaks can help individuals stay present and focused. These practices are known to reduce stress and enhance emotional resilience.

Work-Life Balance: Maintaining a healthy balance between work and personal life is essential. Overcommitting to work at the expense of personal time can contribute to burnout and negative emotions.

Seeking Support: It is important to have a support system, whether it be colleagues, friends, or family. Sharing concerns and seeking advice can provide perspective and alleviate stress.

Positive Affirmations: Incorporating positive affirmations can help counteract negative thoughts. Reminding oneself of strengths and accomplishments can boost confidence and motivation.

Reflective Practices: Regularly reflecting on achievements and learning experiences can foster a positive mindset. Recognizing challenges as opportunities for growth can shift the perspective on difficulties.

Setting Boundaries: Clearly defining work boundaries and knowing when to disconnect is crucial. Overextending oneself can lead to increased stress and negative emotions.

Adapting to Change: Embracing a flexible mindset and adapting to change can reduce resistance to unexpected challenges. Viewing change as a natural part of work can help in managing negative emotions.

Ultimately, understanding one's triggers and developing a personalized toolkit of coping strategies is essential in navigating negative thoughts or emotions while working. It is a continuous process of self-awareness and improvement to create a healthier and more positive work environment.

2. *Do you struggle with maintaining focus and concentration for extended periods?*

Maintaining focus and concentration for extended periods is a common challenge faced by many individuals, particularly in today's fast-paced and technology-driven world. Various factors can contribute to difficulties in staying focused, and understanding and addressing these challenges is essential for productivity and overall well-being.

Digital Distractions: With the prevalence of smartphones, social media, and constant connectivity, digital distractions can significantly impact one's ability to concentrate. Notifications, emails, and online platforms can divert attention, making it difficult to sustain focus on a particular task.

Multitasking: Contrary to popular belief, multitasking can be counterproductive. Juggling multiple tasks simultaneously can lead to divided attention and decreased overall performance.

Fatigue and Sleep Deprivation: Lack of adequate sleep and overall fatigue can significantly impact cognitive function, making it challenging to maintain concentration.

Lack of Interest or Motivation: Engaging in tasks that do not align with personal interests or lack intrinsic motivation can make it difficult to stay focused.

Environmental Factors: Noise, clutter, or uncomfortable workspaces can contribute to distractions and hinder concentration.

Overwhelm and Stress: Excessive workload or tight deadlines can create stress, affecting cognitive performance and focus.

Lack of Routine: Inconsistent schedules and frequent disruptions can disrupt the development of a focused work routine.

Health Factors: Poor physical health, including dehydration or nutritional deficiencies, can impact cognitive function.

Procrastination: Delaying tasks can create a sense of

urgency, leading to rushed and less focused work.

Addressing these factors and adopting strategies to enhance focus can significantly improve one's ability to concentrate for extended periods. It is important to experiment with different approaches and tailor them to individual preferences and work styles for optimal effectiveness.

3. Are your habits and routines aligned with your goals and priorities?

Effective time management is essential for achieving goals and priorities. It involves aligning daily habits and routines with broader objectives to ensure optimal productivity and fulfillment. Assessing whether your habits and routines are in sync with your goals requires introspection and a commitment to intentional planning. Here is how you can develop habits and routines that align with your objectives:

Delegate When Possible: If certain tasks do not align with your core strengths or priorities, consider delegating them to others. Delegation frees up your time for activities that directly contribute to your goals.

Practice Self-Discipline: Cultivate self-discipline to stick to your schedule and resist the temptation to procrastinate. Developing this trait enhances your ability to consistently align your actions with your priorities.

Flexibility and Adaptability: While having a structured schedule is crucial, allow for flexibility to adapt to unforeseen circumstances. A rigid approach may lead to frustration, so be prepared to adjust when necessary.

Self-Care: Include self-care activities in your routine, such as exercise, adequate sleep, and breaks. Taking care of your well-being contributes to sustained energy and focus.

By consciously aligning your habits and routines with your goals, you create a framework that fosters productivity and fulfillment. Regular self-reflection and adjustments will help ensure that your time management strategies remain effective as your goals evolve over time.

Managing internal distractions requires cultivating self-awareness and developing effective coping mechanisms. Techniques such as mindfulness meditation, regular breaks for rejuvenation, and cultivating positive habits can help in maintaining focus and managing distractions.

Additionally, establishing clear goals, prioritizing tasks, and creating structured routines can enhance your self-management abilities and boost productivity.

Meeting Efficiency and Communication Effectiveness

Meetings and poor communication practices can consume a significant amount of time. Evaluate the quality level of your interactions fitting in these categories by using the following questions:

1. Are your meetings often disorganized or lacking a clear agenda?

Meetings that are disorganized or lack a clear agenda can be significant time wasters, contributing to frustration and reduced productivity. Addressing this issue requires thoughtful planning and communication to ensure they serve their intended purpose. Here are several aspects to consider in order to minimize time-wasting in meetings:

Establish Clear Objectives: Clearly define the purpose and objectives of the meeting. This clarity provides a foundation for creating a focused agenda and helps participants understand the goals they need to achieve.

Create a Detailed Agenda: Develop a comprehensive agenda that outlines the topics to be covered, along with designated time slots for each agenda item. Distribute the agenda in advance so that participants can come prepared.

Set Time Limits: Allocate specific time limits to each

agenda item to prevent discussions from dragging on unnecessarily. This encourages participants to stay focused and contributes to a more efficient use of time.

Invite Relevant Participants: Only invite individuals whose presence is necessary for the topics at hand. This helps maintain focus and prevents the meeting from becoming overcrowded with unnecessary attendees.

Pre-Meeting Preparation: Encourage participants to come prepared by reviewing the agenda and any relevant materials beforehand. This ensures that discussions are more informed and decisions can be made efficiently.

Follow-Up on Action Items: Clearly document action items and decisions during the meeting, and follow up with participants afterward to ensure accountability. This prevents the need for revisiting topics in subsequent meetings.

Facilitate Effective Communication: Ensure that there is a clear facilitator or chairperson responsible for guiding the meeting. This person should manage discussions, keep the meeting on track, and encourage active participation.

Use Technology Wisely: Leverage technology tools, such as video conferencing platforms or collaborative documents, to enhance communication and streamline discussions. However, be mindful of potential technical issues that can derail the meeting.

Limit Small Talk: While some social interaction is

valuable, limit unnecessary small talk to ensure that the meeting stays focused on the agenda items. Encourage socializing before or after the official meeting time.

Regularly Review Meeting Effectiveness: Periodically assess the effectiveness of your meetings. Solicit feedback from participants to identify areas for improvement and implement changes accordingly.

Consider Alternatives to Meetings: Evaluate whether a meeting is the most effective way to address certain topics. In some cases, alternative communication methods, such as email updates or collaborative platforms, may be more efficient.

Continuous Improvement: Adopt a mindset of continuous improvement for your meeting processes. Regularly refine your approach based on feedback and changing needs to optimize the use of everyone's time.

By implementing these strategies, you can create a more organized and purposeful meeting environment, reducing the likelihood of time-wasting and ensuring that meetings contribute positively to overall productivity.

2. Do you find yourself attending meetings that are not directly relevant to your work?

Attending meetings that are not directly relevant to your

work can be a common source of time wastage and may impact your overall productivity. It is important to evaluate and manage your participation in meetings to ensure that your time is used efficiently. Here are some considerations and strategies to address this issue:

Delegate Attendance: If the meeting is relevant to your team but not necessarily to your individual role, consider delegating attendance to a colleague who can represent your department. This ensures that the necessary information is still obtained without taking up your valuable time.

Request Agenda in Advance: Ask for the meeting agenda before accepting an invitation. A detailed agenda allows you to gauge the relevance of the topics and make an informed decision about your attendance.

Suggest Alternative Communication Methods: If the meeting's purpose can be achieved through alternative communication methods, such as emails, updates, or collaborative platforms, propose these alternatives to the organizers. This can be more time-efficient for everyone involved.

Prioritize Your Time: Recognize the value of your time and prioritize activities that directly contribute to your work and goals. This may involve making choices about which meetings to attend and which to skip.

By being proactive and intentional about the meetings you attend, you can optimize your time and focus on activities that directly contribute to your work objectives. Open communication with colleagues and management about your priorities and commitments can also contribute to a more streamlined and efficient meeting culture.

3. Are your communication methods efficient, clear, and concise?

Efficient, clear, and concise communication is crucial for effective collaboration and productivity in both professional and personal settings. Ensuring that your messages are well-structured and easily understood can help avoid misunderstandings and streamline workflows. Here are some considerations and strategies for maintaining efficient communication:

Use the Right Medium: Choose the most appropriate communication medium for the situation. While email is suitable for detailed information, quick questions or updates might be better suited for instant messaging or a brief conversation.

Organize Information: Structure your communication logically. Use headings, bullet points, or numbered lists to break down information into digestible chunks. This makes it easier for your audience to follow and understand.

Conciseness Matters: Be concise and get to the point. Avoid unnecessary details that might dilute your message. Respect your audience's time by providing the essential information without unnecessary elaboration.

Active Listening: Communication is a two-way process. Actively listen to others and seek clarification if needed. This helps in avoiding misunderstandings and ensures that your responses are relevant to the context.

Feedback Loop: Encourage open communication by creating a feedback loop. Ensure that there is a mechanism for others to ask questions or seek clarification. This promotes a collaborative and transparent communication environment.

Use Visuals When Appropriate: Incorporate visuals, such as charts or graphs, to convey complex information more efficiently. Visual aids can enhance understanding and retention.

Proofread: Take a moment to proofread your written communication. Correcting spelling and grammatical errors contributes to the professionalism and clarity of your message.

Adaptability: Be adaptable in your communication style. Different situations may require different approaches, and flexibility is key to effective communication.

Continuously refining and honing your communication skills

is an ongoing process. Regularly solicit feedback, reflect on past interactions, and make adjustments as needed to ensure that your communication methods remain efficient, clear, and concise.

Inefficient meetings and ineffective communication can waste valuable time and hinder productivity. To optimize meeting efficiency, establish clear objectives, create structured agendas, and promote active participation.

Additionally, leverage technology tools that facilitate collaborative communication and streamline information exchange. By improving meeting practices and communication effectiveness, you can enhance productivity and ensure that time spent in meetings is purposeful and productive.

By recognizing the limitations of multitasking, managing digital distractions, overcoming procrastination, handling internal distractions, and improving meeting efficiency and communication effectiveness, you can reclaim your time and unlock your productivity potential.

Apply these insights and strategies to cultivate a focused and efficient work environment, enabling you to achieve your goals with greater ease and efficiency.

CHAPTER 3

PRIORITIZING WITH PURPOSE: MASTERING THE ART OF TASK MANAGEMENT

Effective prioritization is the cornerstone of productivity and success. By understanding how to identify and prioritize tasks based on their importance and urgency, you can optimize your workflow, increase efficiency, and achieve your business goals. In this chapter, we will explore assessments, detailed analysis, and practical advice to help you become a master of task management.

Assessing Task Importance and Urgency

To effectively prioritize tasks, it is crucial to evaluate their importance and urgency.

Consider the following questions:

1. Do you have a clear understanding of the importance of each task in relation to your goals?

2. Are you able to identify which tasks require immediate attention and which can be deferred?

3. Do you prioritize tasks based on their potential impact on your business?

Assessing task importance and urgency is a fundamental step in effective task management. By understanding the value and impact of each task, you can make informed decisions about how to allocate your time and resources.

Prioritizing tasks based on their importance ensures that you focus on activities that contribute directly to your business goals. Identifying and addressing urgent tasks in a timely manner helps prevent bottlenecks and allows for a smoother workflow.

By mastering the skill of task assessment, you can lay the foundation for efficient task management.

The Pareto Principle and the 80/20 Rule

As previously seen, the Pareto Principle, also known as the 80/20 Rule, states that approximately 80% of results come from 20% of efforts. Evaluate your understanding and application of this principle with the following questions:

1. Are you aware of the tasks or activities that contribute the most to your business outcomes?

2. Do you allocate a significant portion of your time and resources to the high-impact tasks?

3. Do you regularly analyze and optimize your task allocation based on the 80/20 Rule?

The Pareto Principle reminds us to focus our efforts on the tasks that yield the greatest results.

Identifying the 20% of tasks that generate 80% of the desired outcomes becomes a priority for every project. It enables you to prioritize them and allocate a significant portion of our time and resources to their completion.

Regularly analyzing and optimizing task allocation based on the 80/20 Rule makes it possible for you to maximize productivity and ensure that you are investing your energy in activities that contribute the most value to your business.

Time-Value Matrix

The Time-Value Matrix is a powerful tool for prioritizing tasks based on their urgency and importance. Reflect on the following questions to assess your familiarity with this matrix:

1. Have you used the Time-Value Matrix to categorize and prioritize your tasks?

2. Do you allocate more time to tasks that fall into the "Important and Urgent" quadrant?

3. Do you delegate or eliminate tasks that fall into the "Not Important and Not Urgent" quadrant?

The Time-Value Matrix provides a visual framework for understanding task prioritization. By categorizing tasks into four quadrants:

- Important and Urgent,
- Important but Not Urgent,
- Urgent but Not Important,
- Not Important and Not Urgent

we can allocate our time and resources accordingly. Focusing on tasks that fall into the "Important and Urgent" quadrant helps us address critical issues and avoid crises.

Allocating time for tasks in the "Important but Not Urgent"

quadrant allows for proactive planning and prevents tasks from becoming urgent.

Delegating or eliminating tasks in the "Not Important and Not Urgent" quadrant frees up time for higher-value activities.

By incorporating the Time-Value Matrix into our task management process, we can prioritize effectively and ensure that our efforts align with our business objectives.

Task Dependencies and Sequencing

Understanding task dependencies and sequencing is crucial for effective task management. Evaluate your proficiency in this area with the following questions:

1. Do you consider task dependencies when planning and sequencing your tasks?

2. Are you able to identify tasks that need to be completed before others can begin?

3. Do you utilize tools or techniques to visualize task dependencies and manage their sequencing?

Task dependencies refer to the relationships between tasks, where the completion of one task is dependent on the completion of another. By considering task dependencies and sequencing, we can ensure a smooth workflow and avoid bottlenecks.

Identifying tasks that must be completed before others can begin helps us allocate resources effectively and minimize delays.

Visualizing task dependencies using tools like Gantt charts or project management software provides a comprehensive overview of the project's timeline and aids in managing task sequencing.

Mastery of task dependencies and sequencing allows for efficient task management and promotes productivity.

Advice for the Reader, in summary

To become a master of task management and optimize your productivity, consider the following advice:

1. Assess task importance and urgency to make informed decisions about task prioritization.

2. Apply the Pareto Principle (80/20 Rule) to focus your efforts on high-impact tasks.

3. Utilize the Time-Value Matrix to categorize and prioritize tasks effectively.

4. Consider task dependencies and sequencing to ensure a smooth workflow.

5. Leverage tools and techniques, such as Gantt charts or project management software, to visualize and manage task dependencies.

By implementing these strategies, you can streamline your task management process, increase efficiency, and achieve your business goals effectively.

CHAPTER 4

FROM CHAOS TO CLARITY: ORGANIZING YOUR TIME AND SPACE FOR MAXIMUM EFFICIENCY

In the dynamic world we navigate, the ability to transform chaos into clarity is an invaluable skill. Let's dive into the heart of efficient time and space organization. From the clutter of a chaotic schedule to the disarray of a cluttered workspace, you must explore assessments, and take note of some of our most important advice to guide you on a transformative path toward maximizing efficiency in your personal and professional life.

Gauging Your Current State

Before we embark on the journey of organizing time and space, let's assess your current situation. Reflect on the following questions to gauge the level of chaos in your daily life:

1. How often do you find yourself overwhelmed by the sheer volume of tasks on your to-do list?

This question aims to uncover the frequency and intensity of the feeling of being overwhelmed by tasks. Consider factors such as the complexity of tasks, deadlines, and your ability to manage multiple responsibilities simultaneously. Understanding the degree of overwhelm provides a starting point for addressing time management challenges.

2. Is your workspace cluttered, making it challenging to find what you need quickly?

It has been proven scientifically time and time again that clutter in your workspace can contribute to inefficiency and stress. Consider the physical organization of your desk, files, and digital workspace. A cluttered environment can hinder productivity, and this assessment helps identify areas for improvement.

3. Do you often miss deadlines or appointments due to a lack of organization?

This question forces you to target the impact of disorganization on your ability to meet deadlines and attend appointments. Missing deadlines can lead to stress and affect your professional and personal life. Reflecting on this aspect provides insights into the urgency of improving time management.

4. Are you frequently interrupted or sidetracked during tasks, hindering your productivity?

Interruptions can significantly impact workflow and productivity. Assess how often external factors or distractions divert your attention from tasks. Recognizing patterns of interruption helps in developing strategies to minimize disruptions and maintain focus.

5. Do you feel a sense of stress or anxiety when confronted with a busy schedule?

Stress and anxiety related to a busy schedule can be indicators of time management challenges. Evaluate how your emotional well-being is affected by a packed schedule. Recognizing the emotional toll provides motivation for implementing effective time management strategies.

Take note of your responses to these questions as they will provide a baseline for understanding the areas that need improvement in terms of organization.

The Importance of Organizing Time

Effective time management is the cornerstone of personal and professional success. When time is disorganized, tasks pile up, deadlines are missed, and stress becomes a constant companion. Here is why organizing time is crucial:

Increased Productivity: A well-organized schedule allows for the efficient completion of tasks, leading to increased productivity. Efficient time management allows you to accomplish tasks in a shorter period, maximizing productivity. By prioritizing and focusing on high-impact activities, you ensure that your time is invested in tasks that contribute most to your goals.

Stress Reduction: Knowing what needs to be done and having a plan in place reduces the stress associated with uncertainty and chaos. Having a structured schedule reduces uncertainty and provides a clear roadmap, mitigating stress. When you know what needs to be done and have a plan in place, it alleviates the anxiety associated with disorganization and unpredictability.

Improved Focus: Prioritizing tasks and allocating specific time blocks for different activities enhances concentration. Improved focus leads to better-quality work, and the ability to concentrate on one task at a time boosts overall efficiency.

Enhanced Work-Life Balance: Efficient time management ensures that you allocate time not only for work but also for personal activities, leading to a healthier work-life balance preventing risks such as burnouts.

Accomplishment of Goals: Organized time management facilitates goal-setting and achievement. By breaking down larger goals into smaller, manageable tasks, you create a structured approach to accomplishing both short-term and long-term objectives.

Strategies for Organizing Time

Now, let's dig into strategies to transition from chaos to clarity in your time management:

1. Prioritize Tasks:

   - Assess tasks based on urgency and importance.

   - Use tools like the Eisenhower Matrix to categorize tasks into quadrants.

2. Time Blocking:

   - Allocate specific blocks of time to different tasks or types of work.

- Create a visual schedule to understand how your time is distributed.

3. Set Realistic Goals:

- Break down larger goals into smaller, manageable tasks.

- Ensure that goals are specific, measurable, achievable, relevant, and time-bound (SMART).

4. Use a Calendar System:

- Use digital or physical calendars to track appointments,

deadlines, and events.

- Set reminders to ensure you stay on schedule.

5. Limit Multitasking:

- Focus on one task at a time to enhance concentration and quality of work.

- Multitasking often leads to inefficiency and errors.

6. Establish Routines:

- Create daily or weekly routines for recurring tasks.

- Routines create structure and reduce decision fatigue.

7. Learn to Say No:

- Evaluate commitments before agreeing to them.

- Saying no when necessary protects your time for high-priority tasks.

8. Regularly Review and Adjust:

- Periodically review your schedule and tasks to ensure they align with your goals.

- Be flexible and adjust plans as needed based on changing circumstances.

Evaluating Your Workspace

Now, let's shift our focus to the physical aspect of organization:

your workspace. Reflect on the following questions to assess the state of your workspace:

1. *Is your desk cluttered with papers, documents, or unnecessary items?*

A cluttered desk can contribute to a chaotic and unproductive work environment. Papers and unnecessary items can hinder your ability to find essential tools or documents quickly. This assessment encourages you to evaluate the state of your physical workspace in terms of cleanliness and organization.

2. *Can you easily find the tools and resources you need for your work?*

The efficiency of your work is closely tied to the accessibility of tools and resources. If essential items are difficult to locate, it can lead to frustration and time wastage. This assessment prompts you to consider the accessibility and organization of tools within your workspace.

3. *Do you experience a sense of calm and focus when entering your workspace?*

The emotional impact of your workspace is crucial. A well-organized and tidy workspace contributes to a sense of calm and focus. If entering your workspace induces stress rather than calm, it may indicate the need for organizational improvements.

4. Are there distractions in your environment that hinder your productivity?

Distractions in your physical environment can significantly impact productivity. This can include noise, visual distractions, or interruptions. Recognizing and evaluating these distractions helps in creating a workspace that is conducive to focused work.

5. Does your workspace inspire creativity and motivation?

The aesthetic and functional aspects of your workspace can influence your creativity and motivation. A well-designed workspace that reflects your personality and inspires you can enhance your overall work experience. This assessment encourages you to reflect on the motivational and creative aspects of your workspace.

Your responses will provide insights into the level of organization in your physical workspace, making it possible for you to provide the necessary changes to optimize it.

The Significance of Organizing Space

An organized workspace is more than just a tidy desk; it is a conducive environment for productivity and creativity. Here is why organizing space is essential:

1. Efficiency: An organized space allows you to find what you need quickly, minimizing time wasted on searching for tools or documents.

2. Reduced Stress: Clutter in your physical environment can contribute to mental clutter and stress. An organized space promotes a sense of calm and control.

3. Enhanced Focus: A tidy workspace eliminates distractions, allowing you to concentrate on the task at hand.

4. Improved Workflow: A well-organized space facilitates a smoother workflow, preventing interruptions and bottlenecks.

5. Professional Image: A clean and organized workspace reflects professionalism and attention to detail, which can positively impact your reputation.

Strategies for Organizing Space:
There are many strategies to transform your workspace from chaos to clarity:

1. Declutter Regularly:
   - Remove unnecessary items from your desk and

workspace.

- Regularly declutter to prevent accumulation.

2. Organize Work Zones:

- Create designated zones for different types of work (e.g., a writing zone, a computer work zone).

- Arrange tools and resources based on frequency of use.

3. Use Storage Solutions:

- Invest in storage solutions like shelves, cabinets, or organizers.

- Label storage areas for easy identification.

4. Create a Filing System:

- Implement a filing system for documents, both physical and digital.

- Sort papers into categories and file them accordingly.

5. Digital Organization:

- Organize digital files into folders with clear naming conventions.

- Regularly clean up and organize your computer desktop.

6. Personalize Minimally:

- Personalize your workspace with items that inspire you,

but avoid excessive decorations that can become distracting.

7. Invest in Ergonomics:

- Choose ergonomic furniture and accessories to create a comfortable and efficient workspace.

- Consider the placement of your computer monitor, keyboard, and chair to promote good posture.

8. Manage Cables:

- Use cable organizers to prevent tangling and create a neat appearance.

- Label cables for easy identification.

Reflecting on the Transformation

After implementing these strategies, reflect on the following questions to assess the impact of your efforts:

1. How has your daily schedule changed since implementing time management strategies?

2. Have you experienced a reduction in stress and an increase in productivity?

3. Is your physical workspace more conducive to focused work and creativity?

4. Have you noticed improvements in your ability to find and access tools and resources?

5. How has the transformation from chaos to clarity impacted your overall well-being?

Your reflections will provide valuable insights into the effectiveness of the strategies employed and areas that may require further attention.

The Psychology Behind Organization

Understanding the psychology behind organization is essential for sustaining positive changes. Here are key psychological factors at play:

1. Sense of Control:

- Organization provides a sense of control over your time and environment.
- A perceived lack of control can lead to stress and a feeling of being overwhelmed.

2. Cognitive Load:

- Clutter and disorganization contribute to cognitive load, affecting mental clarity.

- An organized environment reduces cognitive load, freeing up mental resources.

3. Habit Formation:

- Creating and maintaining organizational habits leads to long-term positive changes.

- Consistency is key for habit formation.

4. Environmental Influence:

- The physical environment significantly influences mood and behavior.

- A clean and organized space promotes positive emotions and focus.

5. Motivation and Productivity:

- An organized environment fosters motivation and enhances productivity.

- Achieving small organizational goals can be motivating for larger tasks.

Sustaining Organizational Habits

To sustain the transformation from chaos to clarity, consider the following advice:

1. Consistency is Key:

- Regularly practice time and space organization to reinforce habits.

- Consistency builds a foundation for lasting change.

2. Adapt to Changes:

- Be flexible and adapt your organizational strategies based on evolving needs.

- A one-size-fits-all approach may not be sustainable in the long run.

3. Celebrate Progress:

- Acknowledge and celebrate achievements in your organizational journey.

- Positive reinforcement strengthens your commitment to organizational habits.

4. Seek Professional Help:

- If organization proves challenging, consider seeking assistance from a professional organizer or time management expert.

- Professional guidance can provide personalized strategies for your unique situation.

By assessing your current state, understanding the significance of organization, implementing practical strategies, and reflecting on the psychological aspects, you have taken significant steps toward a more organized and efficient life. Remember, the journey from chaos to clarity is ongoing. Consistently apply the strategies discussed, adapt to changes, and celebrate your progress. As you embrace the psychology behind organization, you empower yourself to navigate life's complexities with clarity, purpose, and efficiency.

CHAPTER 5

HARNESSING THE POWER OF FOCUS: OVERCOMING DISTRACTIONS AND ACHIEVING DEEP WORK

In the digital age, where information bombards us from all directions, the ability to harness the power of focus is a critical skill. Let's focus on the art of overcoming distractions and achieving deep work; a state of intense concentration where productivity and creativity thrive, cultivating a focused mindset in a world filled with distractions.

Evaluating Your Current State of Focus

Reflecting on your current ability to focus is crucial in understanding the challenges and opportunities for improvement. Consider the following assessments:

1. How often do you find your mind wandering during tasks that require concentration?

What is the frequency of your mind wandering away from tasks that demand focused attention. Understanding the prevalence of mental distractions provides insights into potential barriers to sustaining focus.

2. Are external interruptions, such as notifications or background noise, impacting your concentration?

External interruptions can significantly disrupt your ability to concentrate. Assessing the impact of notifications or ambient noise on your focus helps identify external factors that may hinder deep work.

3. Do you often switch between tasks rapidly, or can you sustain attention on one task for an extended period?

Rapid task switching can impede the depth of your work. This question evaluates your ability to sustain attention on a single task over time, providing insights into your capacity for achieving deep work.

4. How frequently do you feel overwhelmed by the sheer volume of information and stimuli in your environment?

Feeling overwhelmed by information overload is a common challenge. The answer to this point helps you dive into the impact of the surrounding environment on your mental state, helping identify areas for improvement.

5. Are you satisfied with the quality and depth of your work, or do you often feel that you could achieve more?

Satisfaction with the quality and depth of your work is a key indicator of focus. Reflecting on your level of contentment provides valuable insights into your current state of achievement and potential areas for enhancement.

The Importance of Focus:

Understanding the significance of focus goes beyond productivity: it is the key to unlocking creativity, innovation, and profound accomplishment. There are five key explanations why cultivating a focused mindset is crucial:

1. Focus is the cornerstone of productivity. It allows you to complete tasks efficiently and with a higher level of accuracy,

minimizing the need for corrections and revisions.

2. Deep work, characterized by sustained focus, leads to the production of high-quality work. It enables you to delve into the intricacies of tasks, resulting in outputs that meet or exceed expectations.

3. Focus is a catalyst for innovation and creativity. In the state of deep work, your mind is free to explore novel ideas and solutions without the constraints of constant distraction.

4. A focused mindset optimizes time usage. When you dedicate undivided attention to a task, you reduce the time needed to complete it, leading to more efficient use of your working hours.

5. Consistent focus contributes to professional growth. It positions you as a reliable and efficient contributor, paving the way for career advancement and recognition.

The Psychology of Focus

Understanding the psychological aspects of focus is crucial for sustained success. Key psychological factors include:

1. Intrinsic Motivation

Intrinsic motivation is a powerful force that propels

individuals to engage in activities for the sheer joy and personal satisfaction derived from the task itself. Unlike extrinsic motivation, which involves external rewards such as money or recognition, intrinsic motivation is an internal drive that comes from within an individual.

At its core, intrinsic motivation is fueled by a genuine interest and passion for the task at hand. When someone is intrinsically motivated, they find fulfillment and gratification in the process of doing the work, irrespective of external outcomes. This internal drive is often associated with a deep sense of purpose, personal values, or an inherent enjoyment of the activity.

The key feature of intrinsic motivation lies in the fact that the activity itself becomes its own reward. This can be particularly potent in enhancing focus and concentration. When individuals are intrinsically motivated, they are more likely to immerse themselves in the task, experiencing a state of flow where time seems to disappear, and their attention is fully absorbed in the activity.

Aligning your work with intrinsic motivations involves a process of self-discovery and reflection. It requires understanding what aspects of a task genuinely interest and fulfill you. This might involve tapping into your passions, recognizing your values, or identifying activities that bring you a sense of accomplishment and joy.

One of the significant advantages of intrinsic motivation is its sustainability. While extrinsic motivators like rewards or praise can lose their effectiveness over time, intrinsic motivation tends to be more enduring. This is because it is rooted in the inherent enjoyment of the task rather than contingent on external factors.

Moreover, tasks that align with intrinsic motivations often lead to a higher quality of work. When individuals are driven by a genuine interest in what they are doing, they are more likely to invest time and effort to hone their skills and produce outcomes of excellence. This intrinsic commitment to mastery contributes not only to personal satisfaction but also to the overall success and effectiveness of the task.

In the professional realm, fostering intrinsic motivation can be a strategic approach to creating a positive and productive work environment. This involves providing employees with opportunities to engage in tasks that align with their personal interests and strengths. Recognizing and acknowledging individual accomplishments and passions can further fuel intrinsic motivation, creating a workplace culture that values not only the results but also the joy derived from the work itself.

Intrinsic motivation is a potent force that goes beyond the

completion of tasks; it enriches the entire experience of work. When individuals align their efforts with what genuinely interests and satisfies them, focus becomes a natural byproduct, leading to enhanced engagement and the achievement of meaningful outcomes.

2. Attention Resilience

Attention resilience stands as a crucial cognitive skill in our modern, information-saturated world. It refers to the capacity to bounce back swiftly from distractions and interruptions, maintaining a focused and undeterred state of attention on the task at hand. In the age of constant stimuli and digital distractions, attention resilience has become a valuable asset, contributing not only to enhanced productivity but also to overall well-being.

This skill is not a fixed trait but rather a trainable and malleable aspect of cognitive functioning. The analogy of resilience is apt here, as attention resilience can be cultivated and strengthened through deliberate practice and the adoption of specific focus strategies.

The regular bombardment of notifications, emails, and other interruptions in our daily lives can fracture our attention, making it challenging to sustain focus on a single task. Attention resilience acts as a shield against this fragmentation, allowing individuals to quickly recover their focus after being momentarily diverted.

Training attention resilience involves the consistent practice of strategies that enhance focus and concentration. Mindfulness meditation, for instance, is a powerful tool that not only improves awareness of the present moment but also hones the ability to redirect attention when it strays. Techniques such as mindful breathing or body scan exercises develop an individual's capability to bring their focus back to the task at hand.

Another effective strategy involves the deliberate use of focused attention intervals, often known as time blocking. By allocating specific periods for deep, undisturbed work and consciously avoiding interruptions during these intervals, individuals can train their minds to resist distractions and build attention resilience over time.

Moreover, the cultivation of a conducive work environment plays a pivotal role in attention resilience. Minimizing external stimuli, creating a dedicated workspace, and employing tools that block out ambient noise contribute to a setting that supports sustained focus and aids in quick recovery from interruptions.

The importance of attention resilience extends beyond the

professional realm; it influences various aspects of life, including learning, relationships, and overall mental well-being. In educational settings, for example, students with robust attention resilience can navigate distractions more effectively, leading to improved academic performance.

In the workplace, fostering a culture that values and supports attention resilience is beneficial for both employees and organizations. This might involve implementing policies that encourage focused work periods, providing training on attention management, or establishing guidelines for effective communication to minimize disruptive interruptions.

Attention resilience is a dynamic and trainable skill that holds significant implications for navigating the demands of our attention-draining environment. By practicing focus strategies, creating conducive environments, and embracing a mindful approach to work, individuals can enhance their attention resilience, ensuring they can quickly recover from distractions and maintain a heightened level of focus and productivity.

3. Goal Alignment

Goal alignment is a powerful principle that acts as a guiding force in enhancing focus and productivity. It involves aligning individual tasks with overarching goals or objectives, creating a seamless connection between daily activities and broader, more strategic aims. This alignment not only provides a sense of purpose but also serves as a compass, directing efforts toward meaningful outcomes.

At its essence, goal alignment is about ensuring that the tasks undertaken on a day-to-day basis contribute directly to the fulfillment of larger, more significant objectives. This connection serves as a motivational force, instilling a sense of purpose and direction in the execution of daily work.

The first aspect of goal alignment involves the clarity of overarching goals. For an individual, team, or organization, having well-defined and clearly communicated goals is essential. These goals could range from personal development milestones to team targets or organizational objectives. When these goals are explicit and understood, they serve as a North Star, providing a clear direction for daily efforts.

Once the overarching goals are established, the next step is to align individual tasks with these objectives. This alignment ensures that every action, project, or assignment contributes meaningfully to the larger picture. It transforms routine tasks from isolated actions into integral components of a grander strategy, fostering a deeper level of engagement and commitment.

The psychological impact of goal alignment is profound.

When individuals can see the connection between what they do every day and the broader objectives they are working towards, it creates a sense of purpose. This sense of purpose is a powerful motivator that goes beyond external rewards or recognition. It taps into intrinsic motivation, fostering a commitment to excellence and a willingness to invest time and effort into the tasks at hand.

Moreover, goal alignment acts as a natural enhancer of focus. Knowing that each task is a building block towards the realization of larger goals sharpens attention. It creates a context for daily activities, emphasizing their importance in the grander scheme of things. This focus is not merely about completing tasks but about achieving outcomes that contribute directly to the success of the overall mission.

In a professional setting, effective goal alignment can significantly impact organizational performance. When teams and individuals are aligned with broader company objectives, it creates a synergistic effect where collective efforts are channeled towards shared goals. This alignment not only improves efficiency but also fosters a collaborative and cohesive work culture.

Goal alignment is a strategic approach to enhancing focus and motivation. By connecting daily tasks to overarching objectives, individuals create a narrative of purpose and significance in their work. This connection serves as a powerful catalyst for sustained effort, improved focus, and the achievement of meaningful outcomes aligned with larger goals.

4. Mindfulness and Present Awareness

In the realm of attention and focus, the practice of mindfulness emerges as a potent tool, particularly through its ability to cultivate present awareness. Mindfulness, rooted in ancient contemplative traditions, has found a profound resonance in modern contexts as a means to counteract the myriad distractions and pressures of contemporary life. At its core, mindfulness is about intentionally paying attention to the present moment without judgment.

Mindfulness practices, such as meditation and mindful breathing, are designed to bring individuals into the present moment. This intentional focus on the 'now' serves as a counterbalance to the inherent tendency of the mind to wander. By being fully present, individuals can harness a heightened sense of awareness, creating a conducive environment for improved focus and concentration.

One of the primary challenges to sustained focus is the wandering nature of the mind. The human mind is naturally inclined to jump between thoughts, memories, and anticipations, often without conscious control. This mental wandering can dilute attention and hinder productivity. Mindfulness acts as a remedy to this cognitive tendency by training individuals to anchor their attention to the present moment.

The practice of mindful breathing is a foundational aspect of mindfulness. By directing attention to the breath, individuals create an anchor that tethers them to the current instant. This focused breathing not only induces a state of relaxation but also serves as a constant point of reference. When the mind starts to drift, returning attention to the breath becomes a simple yet powerful technique to restore present awareness.

The benefits of mindfulness extend beyond the immediate practice. Regular engagement in mindfulness has been linked to neuroplasticity, the brain's ability to reorganize itself. This implies that, over time, the neural pathways associated with attention and focus can be strengthened through consistent mindfulness practices.

Moreover, mindfulness practices foster an attitude of non-judgmental awareness. This means observing thoughts and sensations without assigning value judgments. This quality is particularly relevant to focus enhancement, as it helps individuals disengage from unproductive self-talk or distracting emotions. The mind, liberated from the burden of judgment, becomes a clearer canvas for sustained attention.

In the context of the workplace, introducing mindfulness practices can significantly contribute to a more focused and harmonious work environment. Mindful meetings, for example, can create spaces for undivided attention and more profound engagement in discussions. Companies incorporating mindfulness into their corporate culture often witness improved employee well-being, reduced stress, and increased productivity.

The cultivation of present awareness through mindfulness practices is a transformative approach to improving focus. By training the mind to dwell in the present moment, individuals equip themselves with a powerful antidote to distractions and mental wandering. This heightened awareness not only enhances immediate focus but also contributes to long-term cognitive resilience and well-being.

5. Inhibitory Control

In the web of cognitive functions that contribute to focus, inhibitory control emerges as a critical element. Inhibitory control refers to the cognitive ability to suppress or ignore irrelevant information, impulses, or stimuli, allowing individuals to direct their attention purposefully. This ability to filter out distractions is paramount for maintaining focus and achieving cognitive tasks efficiently.

The cognitive process of inhibitory control is intricately linked to the prefrontal cortex—the executive center of the brain responsible for decision-making, problem-solving, and goal-directed behavior. It acts as a gatekeeper, allowing relevant information to pass through while inhibiting or filtering out irrelevant or distracting inputs. Strengthening inhibitory control is akin to fine-tuning this mental gate, ensuring that attention is directed where it is most needed.

One of the primary challenges to focus is the constant influx of stimuli in our environment. Inhibitory control acts as a cognitive shield, enabling individuals to resist the allure of irrelevant information or distractions. This is particularly crucial in an era where digital devices, notifications, and multitasking can easily fragment attention.

Exercises and strategies designed to enhance inhibitory control play a pivotal role in sharpening focus. Cognitive training activities that involve selectively attending to specific stimuli while ignoring others contribute to the development of inhibitory control. These exercises might include tasks that require individuals to focus on a specific color or shape while disregarding competing stimuli.

The practice of mindfulness, previously discussed, also intersects with inhibitory control. Mindfulness meditation, with its emphasis on non-judgmental awareness and intentional focus, inherently involves the exercise of inhibitory control. As individuals train their minds to return to the present moment, they are, in essence, practicing the suppression of wandering thoughts and distractions.

Moreover, establishing routines and habits can be strategic in fortifying inhibitory control. When certain activities or environments become associated with focused work, the mind learns to inhibit alternative impulses or distractions. This is the essence of habit formation—creating mental shortcuts that guide behavior in alignment with overarching goals, thereby reducing susceptibility to diversions.

In a practical sense, strengthening inhibitory control translates to the ability to resist the pull of instant gratification or immediate distractions. This is particularly relevant in the context of tasks that demand prolonged attention and concentration. By reducing susceptibility to impulses that might lead to multitasking or sidetracking, individuals can maintain a heightened level of focus on the task at hand.

The importance of inhibitory control extends beyond individual productivity; it also influences collaborative efforts. In group settings, individuals with well-developed inhibitory control contribute to a more focused and effective team dynamic. They can navigate discussions and collaborative tasks with a greater ability to filter out extraneous information and maintain a collective focus on shared goals.

Inhibitory control is a cognitive linchpin in the architecture of focus. By honing the ability to suppress irrelevant information and distractions, individuals empower themselves to direct their attention purposefully. Through exercises, mindfulness practices, and the establishment of focused routines, inhibitory control can be strengthened, leading to improved focus and cognitive resilience.

To cultivate and sustain a focused mindset, consider the following:

Begin by incorporating focus strategies in small doses. Gradually increase the duration as you build consistency. Small, consistent efforts lead to lasting habits.

Cultivating a focused mindset is a journey. Be patient with yourself, recognizing that improvement takes time. Celebrate small victories along the way.

It is also vital you understand that adaptability is key. Regularly evaluate the effectiveness of your focus strategies and refine them based on evolving needs and challenges.

As many times as it needs repeating, one of the most crucial parts of being mentally focused is to be physically healthy as well. Physical activity has cognitive benefits. Integrate short breaks of physical movement during deep work sessions to rejuvenate your mind.

It is an art, that of harnessing focus, overcoming distractions, and achieving deep work. By assessing your current state, understanding the significance of focus, implementing practical strategies, and reflecting on psychological factors, you are equipped to cultivate a focused mindset in the midst of a fast-paced world.

As you embark on the journey to harness this power, keep in mind that it is not only about maximizing productivity but also about unlocking your full creative and innovative potential.

CHAPTER 6

THE ART OF SAYING NO: SETTING BOUNDARIES AND PROTECTING YOUR TIME

In the delicate symphony of professional and personal life, a crucial melody emerges: the art of saying no. This nuanced practice is the skillful act of setting boundaries to safeguard one's most precious resource: time. This chapter unfolds the intricacies of saying no, exploring the profound importance of establishing boundaries and navigating the delicate balance between obligations and personal well-being.

Before delving into the art of saying no, let's pause and reflect on our current relationship with commitments.

It is a journey within, a contemplation of how we navigate the various demands on our time and energy.

1. Overwhelm and Emotional Impact:

How frequently do you find yourself overwhelmed by the sheer volume of tasks on your plate? This assessment delves into the emotional impact of your current commitments, exploring the potential mismatch between your capacity and the demands placed on your time.

2. Meeting Deadlines and Practical Challenges:

Are you often unable to meet deadlines or fulfill commitments within the expected timeframe? Struggling to meet deadlines suggests a potential overload of commitments, and this assessment provides insights into the practical challenges associated with your current level of commitment.

3. Saying Yes Out of Obligation:

Do you find yourself saying yes to requests out of obligation rather than genuine interest or alignment with your goals? Saying yes out of obligation can lead to a misalignment between your commitments and your priorities. This assessment explores the motives behind your agreement to various requests.

4. Negative Consequences and Impact on Well-being:

Have you experienced negative consequences, such as burnout or strained relationships, due to an excessive number of commitments? Negative consequences resulting from commitments, like burnout or strained relationships, indicate the potential need for boundary-setting. This assessment helps identify the impact of commitments on your well-being.

5. Balance Between Professional and Personal Commitments:

How satisfied are you with the current balance between your professional and personal commitments? Satisfaction with the balance between professional and personal commitments is a holistic assessment providing insights into whether your current commitments align with your overarching life goals.

Setting boundaries is more than a practical strategy; it is a profound act of self-preservation. It is a shield that protects your mental and emotional well-being, allowing you to focus on meaningful work. It is a way to prevent the draining effects of excessive commitments and to preserve your capacity for focused, meaningful work.

It is important to note that boundaries enable you to focus on high-impact activities. By saying no to non-essential commitments, you create space for deep work and increase your overall productivity and effectiveness.

Not only that, effectively setting a boundary fosters healthier relationships. It allows you to fulfill your commitments with intention and authenticity, leading to more meaningful interactions with others.

Another key aspect that often gets overlooked is that overcommitting is a precursor to burnout. Having the strength to say no to non-essential tasks or favors is a preventive measure, ensuring that you allocate your time and energy in a sustainable manner to avoid exhaustion.

Finally, saying no to conflicting or irrelevant requests ensures that your time is invested in activities that truly matter to you.

Strategies for Saying No and Setting Boundaries

Mastering the art of saying no involves intentional strategies. It is about understanding yourself, your priorities, and communicating effectively.

To convey the right sentiment when answering no to somebody's request, you have to clearly define your personal and professional priorities. This clarity serves as a compass, guiding your decisions and making it easier to discern which commitments align with your goals. The idea being no to sound rude or disinterested, yet using assertive communication to saying no respectfully.

Clearly express your limitations and explain why a particular commitment may not align with your current priorities.

The "No, But" Technique

Instead of a flat-out no, consider using the "No, But" technique. Politely decline the current request and offer an alternative solution or compromise that aligns better with your availability. It is a way to diminish the negative impact perceived on the receiver's end of the no. It can also make you feel better with having to decline their request.

You can also try to communicate your time boundaries to colleagues, friends, and family. Let them know when you are available and when you need focused, uninterrupted time for work or personal activities.

Consider Your Bandwidth

Understand your capacity and bandwidth for taking on new commitments. Saying no is a proactive measure to ensure that your bandwidth is preserved for activities that truly matter.

In addition to this, you can always rely on a strong support system. It is imperative to cultivate one that understands and respects your boundaries. Surrounding yourself with individuals who appreciate your need for balance reinforces your commitment to setting boundaries.

The Psychology of Saying No

Most people think saying no is easy, until they are confronted to a situation where they are required to employ this seemingly devastating answer. Yet, understanding the psychological aspects of saying no is essential for navigating this art effectively. It is all about emotions, empowerment, and building resilience. Answering now has been proven to have many positive cognitive and psychological effects on one's mind and even body.

1. Guilt and Saying No:

Overcoming feelings of guilt associated with saying no requires a shift in mindset. Recognize that saying no is a necessary act of self-care and does not imply a lack of generosity or cooperation.

2. Fear of Missing Out (FOMO):

The fear of missing out can be a barrier to saying no. Reframe your perspective by focusing on the opportunities and experiences that align with your goals rather than succumbing to FOMO.

3. Empowerment through Boundaries:

Setting boundaries is an empowering act. It signifies a conscious choice to prioritize your well-being and goals. Embrace the sense of empowerment that comes with saying no.

4. The Impact on Relationships:

Communicate openly about your boundaries in relationships. Those who respect your boundaries contribute to healthier, more sustainable connections.

5. Building Confidence:

Saying no builds confidence in your ability to make intentional choices. The more you practice setting boundaries, the more confident and assertive you become.

Mastering the Art of Saying No

It seems so simple, yet this answer always comes to lips with so much difficulty. To master the art of saying no and setting boundaries, consider the following. Its wisdom distilled from experience, a guide for the journey.

1. Ensure that your commitments align with your overarching vision for your life. Saying no becomes easier when you recognize the congruence between your choices and your aspirations.

2. Clearly communicate your decisions with respect and

empathy. Providing a transparent explanation, when appropriate, helps others understand your perspective.

3. Be kind to yourself. Recognize that setting boundaries is an act of self-compassion, allowing you to protect your time and energy for activities that truly matter.

4. Connect with individuals who share similar values regarding work-life balance and boundary-setting. Seek support and insights from those who have mastered the art of saying no.

Saying no is not merely a refusal; it is a conscious decision to shape a life that aligns with your values and priorities. As you navigate the delicate balance between obligations and personal well-being, remember that the power of saying no lies not just in the word itself but in the intentional choices it represents.

CHAPTER 7

MAKING TIME FOR WHAT MATTERS: GOAL SETTING AND TIME ALLOCATION STRATEGIES

In the intricate tapestry of our lives, the ability to make time for what truly matters is an invaluable skill. Let's unfurl the art of goal setting and strategic time allocation, I invite you to navigate the labyrinth of priorities and commitments with intention and purpose.

Navigating Your Priorities

Before embarking on goal setting, delve into the foundation: your core values. What principles guide your decisions and aspirations? This introspection lays the groundwork for aligning your goals with your fundamental beliefs.

Ask yourself what do you aspire to achieve in your personal and professional spheres? Identifying these aspirations clarifies the broader direction in which your goals should lead. This assessment sets the stage for more targeted goal setting.

Part of navigating and identifying your priorities is the determine and establish what needs to be set on short-term and long-term.

Goals come in various timelines, and as such, your job is to really find a meaning and path for both paths. Short-term goals provide immediate direction, while long-term goals offer a roadmap for sustained success. Balancing these is key to a holistic approach.

I once wrote about it in my book "100 hours". A particularity of goal-oriented thinking is the ability to assess areas of your personality, your education, and your expertise for growth and improvement. Pinpoint areas in your life that require growth and improvement. Whether personal or professional, recognizing these areas helps set specific goals that contribute to your overall development, and well-being while setting the course towards the fulfillment of these objectives.

Never forget how important your well-being, both mentally and physically, is for the success of your project. As much as you must be well for these goals to be reached, they also have to provide a positive impact on you once accomplished. This is why this way of thinking is a two way street.

Consider the potential impact of your goals on your well-being. Will achieving these goals enhance your overall life satisfaction and happiness? This assessment ensures that your aspirations align with your holistic sense of fulfillment.

The Significance of Goal Setting

Setting goals is not just a task; it's a transformative process that shapes your journey. Remember: it is not about who you are and what you can accomplish by being this person. It is all about who you need to become to reach these objectives. Setting goals is an unavoidable step towards this process. Let's explore the profound significance of goal setting.

Goals provide clarity and direction, acting as beacons guiding your actions. When you have a clear destination, your efforts become purposeful and focused. Everything seem easier, but also structured and organized. You can navigate through your tasks more naturally without having to force yourself and becoming forgetful of the things you would rather avoid doing. This is because they fuel motivation. They create a sense of purpose that propels you forward, even in the face of challenges. The commitment to your goals becomes a driving force in your daily endeavors; and in the complexity of life, decisions abound. Goals act as decision-making anchors, helping you prioritize actions that align with your overarching objectives.

Often times, people will give up due to the fact that despite all the efforts and time and money invested in a new business venture, it seems they are not advancing. Like swimming in the middle of the ocean. Goals provide measurable milestones. Tracking your progress not only keeps you on course but also allows for celebration when you achieve significant milestones. Milestones that can be recorded and measured in time, giving you this sensation that you are not wasting any of these precious seconds the day has to offer.

This is because goal setting enhances time management by providing a framework for prioritization. Tasks that contribute directly to your goals take precedence, optimizing your time allocation.

Strategies for Effective Goal Setting

Embarking on the journey of goal setting requires not just intent but strategic methodologies.

1. SMART Criteria

Adopt the SMART criteria for goal setting: Specific, Measurable, Achievable, Relevant, and Time-Bound. This framework ensures that your goals are clear, achievable, and aligned with your overall vision.

2. Prioritization and Sequencing

Prioritize your goals based on urgency and importance. Sequencing ensures that you tackle tasks in a logical order, creating a seamless flow of progress.

3. Breaking Down Larger Goals

I feel repetition is key fo this point as it is one of the most undervalued advices I used to receive and now give to my clients. Larger goals can be daunting. Break them down into smaller, more manageable tasks. This not only eases the journey but also provides frequent opportunities for accomplishment.

4. Incorporating Milestones

Insert milestones within the timeline of your goals. These checkpoints allow for regular assessment and offer a chance to recalibrate if needed. Not only that, when reached, it gives a reason to celebrate your achievement. If you have a team working on your goals with you, it is a precious moment to demonstrate your appreciation for their hard work, reinforce your ties with them, and also take a step back and appreciate the steps taken up until this point.

Strategic Time Allocation

With goals in place, the next step is the strategic allocation of your most finite resource: time. There is a structured manner in which I like to organize it. And it has been proven over the years to work for most businessmen and women, but also for most people in general.

1. Identifying High-Impact Activities

Assess your goals and identify high-impact activities. These are tasks that contribute significantly to the realization of your objectives. Allocating time to these activities maximizes your efficiency.

2. Creating a Time Budget

Establish a time budget, allotting specific blocks for different activities. This intentional approach ensures that your time aligns with your priorities.

3. Minimizing Time on Low-Priority Tasks

Recognize tasks that, while necessary, are not high-priority. Minimize the time spent on these to free up space for activities that contribute directly to your goals.

4. Utilizing Time Management Techniques

Employ time management techniques such as the Pomodoro Technique or time blocking. These methodologies enhance focus and productivity, making your time allocation more effective.

5. Balancing Work and Personal Time

Striking a balance between work and personal time is crucial. Allocate time for both domains to ensure holistic well-being and prevent burnout.

The Psychology of Goal Setting and Time Allocation

Understanding the psychological aspects of goal setting and time allocation is pivotal in navigating this journey. Two factors are to be taken into consideration: Positive and Negative ones. The motivation associated with fulfilling your goals, and the delays in making them happen because of procrastination, or lack of said motivation.

Having the right amount of motivation plays a crucial role in goal attainment. You have to understand what motivates you and leverage it to propel yourself towards your objectives; or you will fall on the other side of the equation.

Procrastination is a common hurdle. Essentially, it is the lack of motivation, often related to the lack of structured objectives, lack of vision, lack of expertise, lack of tools, and many other reasons that contribute to the ever-decreasing level of motivation you had at the beginning of your endeavor.

Identify its roots and implement strategies to overcome it. This may involve breaking tasks into smaller steps or addressing underlying anxieties.

Advice: Navigating the Landscape of Goals and Time

Embarking on the journey of goal setting and strategic time allocation is a profound endeavor. Consider these pieces of advice as guiding stars in your exploration. Each one comes from personal experience and has been confirmed by successful friends, business partners, clients and other high net-worth acquaintances.

1. Align Goals with Your Vision

Ensure that your goals align harmoniously with your overarching vision. This alignment provides a sense of purpose, making the pursuit of your goals a meaningful journey.

2. Embrace Adaptability

Embrace adaptability in the face of changing circumstances. Life is dynamic, and the ability to adjust your goals and time allocation ensures resilience and continued progress. Without flexibility you can never be competitive or react fast enough to change, which is one of the main reasons of failures in the early stages of new companies.

3. Celebrate Milestones Along the Way

Celebrate milestones, regardless of their size. Each accomplishment is a testament to your dedication and effort. Celebrations fuel motivation for the next leg of your journey.

4. Balance Ambition with Realism

Balance ambition with realism. While aiming high is admirable, setting realistic goals ensures that they remain achievable and sustainable in the long run.

5. Prioritize Your Well-being

Prioritize your well-being in the pursuit of goals. A healthy, balanced life is the foundation for sustained success and fulfillment.

As you navigate the landscape of your priorities, remember that the art lies not just in setting goals but in the intentional allocation of your most precious resource: time. Never forget: Time is the only currency we can never have enough, or more, of.

CHAPTER 8

BUILDING ROUTINES AND RITUALS: ESTABLISHING HABITS FOR SUSTAINABLE TIME MANAGEMENT

In the dynamic interplay of daily life, the establishment of routines and rituals emerges as a cornerstone for sustainable time management. Here lies the importance of building routines and rituals, and these next pages are inviting you to embark on a journey that fosters habits conducive to long-term efficiency and well-being.

Before getting started with the benefits, let's clarify a few of the most important terms. Routines and rituals, while often used interchangeably, hold distinct meanings.

Routines are consistent patterns of behavior, while rituals are symbolic actions imbued with significance.

We will explore how both contribute to effective time management on their own right. To get started you will need to reflect on your daily patterns: Are there recurring activities that naturally form a part of your day? Identifying these patterns forms the initial step in crafting purposeful routines and rituals.

Understand why these patterns of behavior are essential for cognitive and emotional well-being. There is a whole universe of reasons behind every behavior, every habit, every belief, and every decision people make every day. I recommend you take notes in the most honest manner possible about your own patterns with the sole intent of unraveling the psychology of all your character strengths and flaws.

One of the goals of this exercise is to find the negative patterns and habits you can correct in order to free more time, mind space and restructure your daily life to become more efficient with your goals previously established.

Balancing Flexibility and Structure

Striking a balance between flexibility and structure is key. Routines provide structure, while rituals add a touch of personalization. This equilibrium ensures that your habits adapt to the evolving nature of life.

The Importance of Building Habits

Understanding why habits matter is crucial for appreciating the impact of routines and rituals on sustainable time management.

In the same way an industrial machine is efficient because it is automated and works flawlessly with a specific purpose, your life and work will benefit from the schematics of this concept. In a person, they are called habits.

Habits automate tasks, reducing the cognitive load associated with decision-making. This automation enhances efficiency, allowing you to navigate daily responsibilities with greater ease.

By successfully building habit, a positive consequence emerges within each individual. This is what is called "Conserved mental energy".

The conservation of mental energy is a byproduct of habits. By establishing routines, you conserve mental energy for more complex and creative tasks, contributing to heightened overall productivity.

This allows you to have the strength, time and mind space to build a framework for success. When positive behaviors become ingrained, they lay the groundwork for achieving larger goals. Said strength can also be called resilience.

Resilience is cultivated through habits. Consistent patterns of behavior foster adaptability and perseverance, essential qualities for navigating challenges and setbacks.

Strategies for Building Effective Routines and Rituals

The journey of habit formation requires strategic planning and intentional choices.

1. Start Small and Gradual

Begin the journey of habit formation with small, manageable steps. Gradual integration ensures that habits are sustainable and not overwhelming.

An advice I wish I had received before I began my entrepreneurial journey: Never compare yourself to someone who is already much more successful than yourself. Visualize where they come from instead. And appreciate the years of hardship they endured and navigated through to be where they are today. They started at the same point as you.

2. Align with Personal Values

Ensure that your routines and rituals align with your personal values. Habits grounded in values are more likely to endure and contribute to a sense of purpose.

3. Create a Ritualized Environment

Designate specific spaces for your rituals. Creating a ritualized environment enhances the symbolic significance of these actions, making them more impactful.

4. Attach New Habits to Existing Routines

Facilitate habit adoption by attaching new behaviors to existing routines. This association streamlines the integration process and enhances the likelihood of success.

Nurturing Consistency and Adaptability

Consistency is the bedrock of effective routines and rituals. Embrace flexibility in routine adherence. Life is dynamic, and flexibility ensures that your habits remain adaptable to changing circumstances. Never get stuck in your ways, this would mean having developed a comfort zone from which there is no escape. Having a safety zone is normal and mandatory, you cannot live constantly on edge, however establishing a full out comfort zone would mean not being able to keep growing, evolving, taking risks, and that is where dreams come to die.

To ensure a safety zone does not get converted into a comfort zone, you need to be accountable for your actions. Accountability is a powerful tool in habit formation. Whether through self-accountability or involving a trusted ally, explore how accountability reinforces consistent behavior. Either you or a third party will be keeping you in check and making sure you don't rest on your laurels, but don't make rash decisions either while building your habits and rituals in and out of your safety zone.

The Psychology of Building Habits

Understanding the psychological underpinnings of habit formation is integral to nurturing lasting change.

1. Cue-Routine-Reward Loop

Explore the cue-routine-reward loop—the psychological mechanism behind habit formation. Understanding this loop empowers you to intentionally design habits that endure.

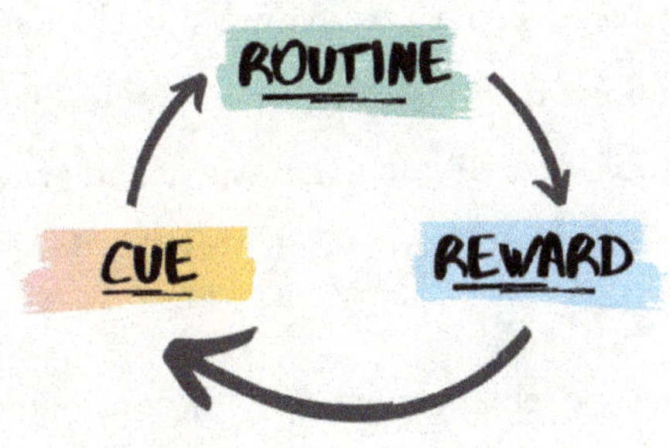

2. Overcoming Resistance

It is in our nature to resist to change. Because change can mean diving into the unknown, the unfamiliar, taking risks... Resistance is a common hurdle in habit formation. Find the strategy that fits your personality that will make you overcome resistance, whether internal or external, to foster lasting change.

3. Incorporating Positive Reinforcement

Positive reinforcement is a potent tool in habit building. Learn how to incorporate positive reinforcement to solidify habits and make them enjoyable.

4. Transformative Impact on Mindset

As I have said repeatedly, having success in life or work does not depend on who you are. It has everything to do with who you have to become in order to be in the right mind and position to earn that success. That is why habit formation extends beyond behavior. It transforms your mindset. Developing routines and rituals contribute to a positive and growth-oriented mindset when guided by the right goals, visions and even mentors.

Your identity is closely intertwined with your habits. Be aware that habit formation shapes your identity and influences the narrative you tell yourself. Make sure to set yourself on the right path, always focusing on the end result, the final goal that motivated to get started in the first place.

Advice: Nurturing Sustainable Habits

Embarking on the journey of building routines and rituals requires patience and mindful cultivation. Consider these pieces of advice as companions on your path.

1. Start with Intent

Initiate the journey with intent. Clearly define the purpose behind each habit, ensuring that they align with your overarching goals.

2. Embrace Progress, Not Perfection

Embrace progress over perfection. Habits are a continual journey of growth. Celebrate each step forward, acknowledging that perfection is not the goal.

3. Build Habits Gradually

Adopt habits gradually. Rather than overwhelming yourself with numerous changes, focus on building one habit at a time. This approach fosters sustainable integration.

4. Cultivate Self-Compassion

Cultivate self-compassion in the face of setbacks. Habits may falter, but a compassionate approach allows you to regroup and continue forward.

5. Infuse Joy into Rituals

Infuse joy into your rituals. The more enjoyable and meaningful these practices are, the more likely they are to become enduring habits.

As you navigate the realm of habit formation, remember that the essence lies not just in the actions themselves but in the intentional meaning you infuse into each routine and ritual.

CHAPTER 9

FROM PROCRASTINATION TO ACTION: OVERCOMING RESISTANCE AND BOOSTING MOTIVATION

In the beautiful dance of productivity, we embark on a profound journey from the clutches of procrastination towards the liberating realm of action, peeling back the layers of this complex dynamic. Procrastination, that elusive adversary lurking in the shadows of productivity, conceals deeper roots, and understanding its multifaceted nature requires a nuanced exploration of the psychological threads that contribute to the delay in taking action.

Understanding the Nature of Procrastination:

Procrastination, the silent adversary of productivity, often conceals deeper roots. Reflect on the reasons why you cannot gather the strenght, or motivation, our courage, or whatever you lack of in order to get started on the task you are avoiding to perform. Many factors can be a reason such as:

- Fear

- Perfectionism

- Lack of motivation

- Lack of structure

- Overwhelming tasks (may it be in quantity or size)

Be as honest as you can to figure the root cause of the problem, and deal with it accordingly.

Procrastination is a uniquely individual journey, a dance with personal triggers that often remain veiled. Whether rooted in the fear of failure, a lack of clarity, or the demanding specter of perfectionism, identifying these triggers becomes a compass, guiding the formulation of targeted strategies to overcome this formidable hurdle. The mindset, be it fixed or growth-oriented, casts a significant influence on procrastination, dictating both the propensity to defer tasks and the ability to triumph over this challenge.

Guilt, a faithful companion to procrastination, often forms a detrimental cycle that exacerbates the struggle. This chapter seeks to unravel the interplay between guilt and delayed action, providing insights into breaking free from this self-perpetuating loop. Moreover, it delves into the concept of procrastination as a potential coping mechanism and suggests healthier alternatives to address the underlying issues that may contribute to this behavior.

Practical strategies are indispensable in the battle against procrastination. The art of breaking tasks into micro-steps emerges as a potent technique, transforming overwhelming endeavors into manageable components. Time-blocking, another powerful strategy, involves the allocation of specific time slots to tasks, creating a structured approach that minimizes the allure of procrastination by rendering tasks more tangible and less abstract.

Setting realistic goals stands as a cornerstone in overcoming procrastination. The allure of unrealistic goals often becomes fertile ground for procrastination, making it imperative to set objectives that are not only challenging but also achievable, thereby contributing to consistent progress. The establishment of accountability structures, whether through self-accountability techniques or by involving external sources, emerges as a formidable ally in the fight against procrastination, providing checks and balances that foster consistency and commitment.

Motivation, the driving force behind purposeful endeavors, is a complex amalgamation of intrinsic and extrinsic factors, each playing a unique role in kindling the flames of action. Cultivating a growth mindset becomes pivotal in the motivational journey. This mindset, characterized by a belief in one's capacity for growth and development, serves as a powerful catalyst for proactive steps and resilience in the face of challenges. Aligning goals with overarching objectives emerges as another influential factor, providing a sense of purpose that makes each action a meaningful step towards a larger, more significant vision.

Celebrating progress, irrespective of its scale, unveils itself as a potent motivational tool. Small victories, when acknowledged and celebrated, create positive feedback loops that fuel a continuous cycle of motivation and action. The significance of progress, no matter how incremental, lies in its ability to build momentum and sustain the drive towards larger goals.

Embarking on the journey from procrastination to action demands not just strategies but a compass and guiding principles. The cultivation of a proactive mindset, the leverage of visualization as a tool for motivation, the building of momentum with small wins, the seeking of support and accountability, and the regular reflection on motivational factors stand as pillars of guidance on this transformative path.

Advice for Conquering Procrastination and Cultivating Motivation

Embarking on the journey from procrastination to action requires guidance and steadfast commitment. Consider these pieces of advice as companions on this transformative path.

Develop a Proactive Mindset:

Cultivate a proactive mindset. Shifting from reactive to proactive thinking lays the groundwork for overcoming procrastination and embracing a more action-oriented approach.

Leverage the Power of Visualization:

Visualization is a tool for motivation. Envisioning the successful completion of tasks enhances motivation and serves as a mental rehearsal for action.

Build Momentum with Small Wins:

Build momentum with small wins. Tackling manageable tasks initially creates a positive trajectory, gradually eroding the inertia associated with procrastination.

Seek Support and Accountability:

Seek support from others. Engage in accountability partnerships or share your goals with someone trustworthy. The supportive environment enhances motivation and commitment.

Reflect on Motivational Factors:

Regularly reflect on motivational factors. What inspires and drives you? Understanding these factors fortifies your arsenal against procrastination.

CHAPTER 10

THE TIME-PRODUCTIVITY CONNECTION: UNDERSTANDING THE SCIENCE OF PEAK PERFORMANCE

In the sensual choreography of productivity, Time, the currency of productivity, emerges as a finite resource, and unraveling the art of harnessing it effectively becomes the linchpin for unlocking unparalleled levels of performance and efficiency.

The Core of Temporal Influence in Productivity

Time, a constant yet subject to diverse perceptions and applications, is explored philosophically and psychologically when it comes to personal and professional growth. It points at how individuals perceive and ascribe value to this finite resource. Understanding the concept of temporal boundaries is akin to deciphering the philosophical and psychological dimensions of time. It involves an exploration of how time, often considered an immutable constant, is subject to the subjective interpretations and psychological nuances of individuals.

The significance lies in recognizing that perceptions of time plays a pivotal role in shaping our approach to productivity.

By understanding the varied perspectives people have regarding time, one can develop strategies that resonate with these perceptions, fostering a more effective and harmonious relationship with this finite resource.

Temporal Harmony with Productivity:

Foundational to productivity is the symbiotic dance between time and efficiency. The key relationship between time management and optimal efficiency recognizes that time is not merely a chronological measure but a dynamic force influencing productivity. Effective time management becomes the catalyst for heightened productivity and, conversely, increased productivity can, in turn, impact the judicious use of time. By understanding and harnessing this reciprocal influence, people can embark on a journey towards achieving a harmonious balance, where time becomes a facilitator rather than a constraint in the pursuit of peak performance.

Temporal Prowess for Optimal Performance:

Time serves as the catalyst for optimal performance. Grasping the art of optimizing and judiciously allocating time sets the stage for achieving peak productivity, paving the way for an enriched journey.

Temporal prowess for optimal performance involves recognizing time as a dynamic force that propels individuals towards their peak capabilities. It goes beyond viewing time as a mere constraint and instead positions it as a powerful catalyst for achieving optimal performance. Successful people understood to treat time not as a passive resource but as an active agent in the journey towards peak productivity. By mastering this temporal prowess, entrepreneurs can unlock unparalleled levels of performance and efficiency, propelling themselves towards a fulfilling and enriched professional and personal journey.

Psychology Governing Temporal Perception

The psychology governing temporal perception lies into the intricate ways in which individuals perceive and experience time, exploring the cognitive and emotional factors that shape our understanding of this abstract concept. It is a captivating exploration that goes beyond the mere ticking of a clock, unraveling the complex interplay between the human mind and the passage of time.

Temporal perception is inherently subjective, shaped by a myriad of psychological elements. One crucial aspect is the influence of cognitive processes on our perception of time. The brain processes temporal information in a non-linear fashion, meaning that our perception of time can vary based on the complexity of cognitive activities. When engaged in challenging or novel tasks, time may appear to pass more slowly as the brain dedicates more resources to processing information. Conversely, during routine or monotonous activities, time may seem to fly by as the brain operates on autopilot.

Emotions also play a pivotal role in shaping how we perceive time. Emotional states, such as stress, anxiety, or excitement, can distort our temporal judgments. For instance, moments of intense stress may feel prolonged, creating a sense of time dilation, while moments of joy or excitement may seem to pass in the blink of an eye. The psychological impact of emotions on temporal perception highlights the relationship between our mental states and the ticking of the clock.

Cultural and individual differences further contribute to the complexity of temporal perception. Cultures with a strong emphasis on punctuality and adherence to schedules may instill a heightened awareness of time in individuals from those cultures. Moreover, personal experiences, memories, and age can shape temporal perception. As individuals age, the sensation that time is passing more quickly often emerges, a phenomenon known as time compression.

Understanding the psychology governing temporal perception has profound implications for various aspects of life, including productivity, decision-making, and overall well-being. In the realm of productivity, individuals can optimize their time management strategies by acknowledging the impact of cognitive load on temporal perception. Employing techniques that enhance focus and engagement can create a more accurate subjective experience of time, leading to improved efficiency.

In decision-making, awareness of temporal biases can foster more informed choices. For instance, individuals may be prone to underestimating the time required for a task, leading to procrastination or rushed efforts. By understanding these biases, individuals can make adjustments to their planning and decision-making processes, mitigating the effects of temporal distortions.

The psychology governing temporal perception also intersects with mindfulness practices. Mindful awareness encourages individuals to be present in the moment, fostering a deeper connection with the passage of time. By cultivating mindfulness, individuals can develop a more balanced and intentional relationship with time, reducing the impact of stress-induced temporal distortions.

In essence, the psychology governing temporal perception is a multifaceted exploration into the subjective experience of time. It invites us to appreciate the ways in which our minds navigate the temporal landscape, offering insights that extend beyond the quantifiable measurements on a clock. By unraveling the complexities of temporal perception, individuals can harness this understanding to enhance various aspects of their lives, creating a more harmonious relationship with the ever-flowing river of time.

Chronotypes and Circadian Rhythms Demystified:
Chronotypes and circadian rhythms are intricate elements that contribute significantly to our daily lives, influencing our energy levels, cognitive functions, and overall well-being. Demystifying these concepts involves understanding the biological intricacies that govern our internal clocks and the profound impact they

have on our daily activities.

1. Chronotypes

Chronotypes refer to individual variations in circadian rhythms, determining the time of day when a person is most alert, energetic, and productive. There are three primary chronotypes: morning, evening, and intermediate types. Morning chronotypes, often referred to as "morning larks," experience peak alertness and energy levels early in the day. Evening chronotypes, known as "night owls," reach their peak later in the day. Intermediate types fall somewhere between these extremes. Demystifying chronotypes involves recognizing that these preferences are not just personal habits but are deeply rooted in our biological makeup.

Understanding chronotypes can significantly impact daily productivity. For instance, aligning tasks with one's chronotype can enhance efficiency and quality of work. Night owls might find that their creative energy peaks in the evening, making it ideal for tasks requiring innovation.

Morning larks, on the other hand, may excel at activities demanding focus and attention early in the day. By demystifying chronotypes, individuals gain insights into their optimal periods of alertness and can strategically plan their daily schedules for heightened productivity.

2. Circadian Rhythms:

Circadian rhythms are the natural, internal processes that regulate the sleep-wake cycle and repeat roughly every 24 hours. These rhythms are influenced by external factors such as light and darkness, with the master clock located in the brain's hypothalamus orchestrating various bodily functions. Demystifying circadian rhythms involves recognizing the subtle dance of hormones like melatonin and cortisol, which play pivotal roles in regulating sleep, alertness, and overall physiological well-being.

The circadian rhythm peaks during the day, promoting wakefulness and alertness, and reaches its lowest point during the night, facilitating restorative sleep. Demystifying circadian rhythms involves understanding that disruptions to this natural cycle, such as irregular sleep patterns or exposure to artificial light at night, can have profound effects on health and productivity. For instance, individuals working against their natural circadian rhythm may experience challenges in maintaining optimal focus and cognitive performance.

Aligning daily activities with circadian rhythms can lead to enhanced overall well-being. Demystifying circadian rhythms allows individuals to make informed decisions about when to engage in specific activities. For example, recognizing the importance of a consistent sleep schedule aligned with one's circadian rhythm can improve the quality of sleep and, consequently, daytime alertness and productivity.

In essence, demystifying chronotypes and circadian rhythms empowers individuals to optimize their daily routines, aligning activities with their natural biological preferences. This understanding goes beyond a simple acknowledgment of morning or evening preferences; it delves into the intricate science behind our internal clocks, offering a roadmap for enhanced productivity, improved sleep quality, and overall better health.

Attaining the Flow State: The Pinnacle of Productivity

The flow state, often referred to as "being in the zone," is a psychological phenomenon characterized by an individual's complete absorption and optimal performance in a specific task. Achieving the flow state involves a deep sense of focus, heightened concentration, and a seamless, almost effortless, connection between actions and awareness. Decoding the flow state involves unraveling the elements that contribute to this highly sought-after mental state and understanding how individuals can cultivate an environment conducive to its occurrence.

One of the key aspects of the flow state is the merging of action and awareness, where individuals become fully immersed in the task at hand. Time seems to distort, with individuals often reporting a sense of time passing differently or even standing still. This distortion arises from the intense concentration on the present moment, resulting in a state where individuals are completely absorbed in the activity, losing track of external factors.

The balance between challenge and skill is a fundamental component of entering the flow state. When the challenge of a task aligns with an individual's skill level, a sweet spot is reached, creating an optimal balance. Tasks that are too easy may lead to boredom, while tasks that are too challenging can result in anxiety or frustration. Decoding the flow state involves identifying activities that match one's skill level and present a moderate level of challenge, stimulating a sense of engagement without overwhelming the individual.

Eliminating distractions is crucial for entering and sustaining the flow state. Distractions disrupt the seamless focus required for optimal performance. Whether external interruptions or internal thoughts, distractions can pull individuals out of the flow state. Decoding this aspect involves creating an environment that minimizes disruptions, allowing individuals to maintain deep concentration and sustained attention on the task.

The neurochemistry behind the flow state adds another layer to its decoding. Neurotransmitters such as dopamine and norepinephrine play a significant role in achieving and sustaining the heightened level of productivity associated with the flow state. These neurotransmitters are linked to pleasure, reward, and arousal, creating a neurochemical cocktail that enhances motivation and focus. Understanding this neurochemistry sheds light on why individuals often describe the flow state as an intrinsically rewarding and enjoyable experience.

Cultivating an environment that fosters the flow state involves recognizing the conditions that facilitate its occurrence. Clear goals and immediate feedback are essential elements. Individuals need to have a clear understanding of what they are trying to achieve, allowing for a sense of purpose and direction. Immediate feedback provides real-time information about progress, enabling individuals to make quick adjustments and maintain momentum.

Decoding the flow state involves understanding the delicate interplay of psychological and neurobiological factors that contribute to this unique state of consciousness. By balancing challenge and skill, eliminating distractions, and leveraging the neurochemistry of motivation, individuals can create conditions that enhance the likelihood of entering the flow state.

Cultivating an environment conducive to flow not only leads to peak performance but also fosters a deeply satisfying and fulfilling engagement with tasks and activities.

CHAPTER 11

TIME AS A RESOURCE: LEVERAGING TECHNOLOGY AND TOOLS FOR TIME OPTIMIZATION

In the multifaceted role of time as a resource, let's explore the art of harnessing technology and tools for optimal time management. In this digital era, where time is both a commodity and a challenge to manage, understanding how to leverage advancements in technology becomes paramount for effective time optimization.

The Evolving Landscape of Time Management

The integration of technology into our daily lives has ushered in a transformative shift in the way we perceive and manage time. This evolution marks a significant departure from traditional methods, introducing a dynamic and interconnected digital landscape that profoundly impacts our relationship with time and productivity.

In this era of digital transformation, the boundaries between personal and professional spheres are becoming increasingly blurred. The omnipresence of technology has not only redefined how we engage with information but has also revolutionized our approach to time management. The once-clear delineation between work and personal life has given way to a more fluid and integrated existence, where the tools we use for personal productivity seamlessly intersect with those tailored for professional tasks.

This transformation brings forth both challenges and opportunities. On one hand, the digital age presents a plethora of potential distractions, ranging from incessant notifications to the allure of social media. These distractions can erode focus and disrupt the traditional rhythms of productivity. On the other hand, technology offers unprecedented opportunities to enhance efficiency and organization. The digital toolbox now includes a variety of task and project management apps, calendar and scheduling tools, note-taking and information management systems, as well as communication and collaboration platforms.

Navigating this digital toolbox is crucial for effective time management. Task and project management apps have become keystones, facilitating streamlined organization of tasks and collaborative project efforts. Calendar and scheduling tools have evolved beyond simple date marking, now offering features that enable smart scheduling and time-blocking techniques. Information overload, a common challenge in the digital age, is addressed through innovative note-taking and information management systems, providing a structured means to organize scattered thoughts and details. Communication and collaboration platforms bridge the gap in an interconnected world, ensuring seamless interaction without compromising time efficiency.

As the landscape continues to evolve, technology emerges not only as a facilitator of time management but also as a strategic partner in optimizing our use of time. Automation, once a futuristic concept, has become a powerful ally in time optimization, allowing for the automation of repetitive tasks and reducing the risk of errors.

Smart devices and wearables have transitioned from novelty to essential tools, transforming how we engage with our daily schedules and tasks. Data analytics, once the domain of big businesses, is now harnessed at an individual level, providing valuable insights into personal productivity and prompting informed adjustments.

However, with the integration of technology comes the imperative to safeguard sensitive information. Security and privacy considerations become paramount, ensuring that the benefits of time optimization through technology are not compromised by data vulnerabilities.

In essence, the evolving landscape of time management is characterized by a delicate balance between the challenges posed by digital distractions and the opportunities presented by innovative technological tools. As individuals navigate this dynamic terrain, the ability to harness the benefits of technology while mitigating its potential pitfalls becomes a critical skill. The ongoing journey through this evolving landscape necessitates adaptability, continuous learning, and a mindful approach to technology usage, ensuring that our relationship with time remains not only efficient but also purposeful.

Navigating the Digital Toolbox

In the contemporary landscape of time management, effective navigation of the digital toolbox has become instrumental in optimizing productivity and efficiency. This toolbox, comprised of an array of technological applications and platforms, offers a diverse set of tools designed to streamline tasks, enhance collaboration, and provide innovative solutions to the challenges presented by the digital age.

Task and project management apps stand as pivotal components within the digital toolbox. These applications, such as Asana, Trello, or Monday.com, provide individuals and teams with the ability to organize tasks, track progress, and foster collaboration in a centralized digital space. For instance, Trello employs boards, lists, and cards to help users visually organize their projects, making it an invaluable tool for task management.

Calendar and scheduling tools, another integral aspect of the digital toolbox, have evolved beyond basic date-marking functions. Platforms like Google Calendar or Microsoft Outlook offer features that enable smart scheduling and time-blocking techniques. For example, Google Calendar allows users to set goals, which the application then intelligently schedules into available time slots, promoting a more efficient use of time.

In addressing the challenge of information overload, innovative note-taking and information management systems have emerged. Evernote and Microsoft OneNote, for instance, provide users with digital notebooks, allowing them to organize thoughts, ideas, and important details in a structured manner.

These tools empower individuals to declutter their mental space and access information seamlessly, enhancing overall productivity.

Communication and collaboration platforms play a vital role in fostering connectivity in an interconnected world. Tools like Slack or Microsoft Teams not only facilitate real-time communication but also offer features that promote collaborative work environments. Slack, with its channels and direct messaging, creates a space for efficient communication, reducing the need for lengthy email exchanges and fostering a more dynamic collaboration process.

As technology continues to advance, the integration of automation has become a powerful strategy for time optimization. Automation tools like Zapier or IFTTT enable individuals to create workflows that automatically execute repetitive tasks. For instance, an individual could set up an automation to save email attachments to cloud storage, reducing the manual effort required for such routine actions.

Smart devices and wearables, including smartphones, smartwatches, and voice-activated assistants, have transformed how individuals engage with time management. Smartwatches, such as the Apple Watch or Fitbit, not only monitor schedules but also provide notifications and reminders, keeping users informed and on track with their daily activities. Voice-activated assistants like Amazon's Alexa or Apple's Siri offer hands-free ways to set reminders, check schedules, or even draft messages, contributing to a more seamless integration of technology into daily life.

Data analytics, once confined to the realm of big businesses, has become a tool for individual productivity. Apps like RescueTime or Toggl Track analyze digital footprints and usage patterns, providing insights into time management habits. For example, RescueTime categorizes time spent on different applications and websites, offering a visual representation of how time is allocated, which users can leverage for informed adjustments to their routines.

However, amid the benefits of technology integration, considerations of security and privacy become paramount. As individuals utilize these digital tools to optimize their time, maintaining the confidentiality and integrity of sensitive information is essential. This emphasizes the need for adopting secure practices, utilizing encrypted platforms, and staying vigilant against potential cyber threats.

Navigating the digital toolbox involves strategically leveraging a range of technological tools to enhance time management. From task and project management apps to communication platforms, automation tools, and data analytics, the digital toolbox provides a diverse set of solutions. Effectively using these tools requires a mindful approach, aligning them with individual needs and goals while remaining vigilant about security and privacy considerations. As technology continues to evolve, the ability to navigate this digital landscape becomes a key determinant in achieving optimal productivity and efficiency.

The Human Touch in a Digital World

In the era of advanced technology and digital integration, the importance of maintaining the human touch in our interactions and decision-making processes cannot be overstated. While technology provides powerful tools for efficiency and productivity, the nuanced aspects of human judgment, mindfulness, and continuous learning remain essential for a holistic and meaningful approach to time management.

1. Balancing Human Judgment and Technology

Despite the capabilities of technology, human judgment remains irreplaceable. The ability to interpret context, understand emotions, and make nuanced decisions based on experience and empathy is a uniquely human trait. Striking the right balance between leveraging technological capabilities and applying human judgment is crucial. For example, in project management, while project management tools like Jira or Asana facilitate task tracking, it requires human judgment to prioritize tasks based on strategic importance and team dynamics.

2. Mindful Technology Usage

Mindful technology usage is a key aspect of maintaining the human touch in a digital world. This involves cultivating an awareness of how technology is being used, setting intentional boundaries, and avoiding mindless consumption. Techniques such as digital detox, where individuals consciously disconnect from devices for a specified period, contribute to a healthier relationship with technology. By fostering a mindful approach, individuals can ensure that technology enhances their lives without overwhelming them.

3. Continuous Learning in the Digital Sphere

In a rapidly evolving digital landscape, the commitment to continuous learning becomes paramount. Embracing new technologies, staying informed about updates and advancements, and adapting to changing digital trends are essential components of effective time management. Platforms like LinkedIn Learning or Coursera provide opportunities for continuous skill development. By embracing a mindset of perpetual learning, individuals can stay ahead of the curve and make informed decisions about the integration of new technologies into their time management practices.

The human touch in a digital world extends beyond the use of technology to the way individuals interact with each other. Personal connections, effective communication, and collaboration fostered by human relationships remain vital components of a well-rounded approach to time management.

As individuals navigate the complexities of the digital landscape, the integration of technology should enhance rather than replace the human touch. The delicate equilibrium between leveraging technological tools and preserving human-centric values ensures that time management remains not only efficient but also meaningful.

ABOUT THE AUTHOR

Damien Soitout is a French businessman, investor and philanthropist.

He is the owner of the CPF Group based in the US, France and Mexico, with experience, expertise and success in 9 industries.

He has worked with some of the largest groups in the world, and has supported thousands of entrepreneurs and dreamers achieve their professional and personal goals through personalized programs, consulting, and free online content.

One of his missions is to open the minds of people with ambitious goals to organize their projects in such a way that they do not risk paying the
Dumb Tax.